150

SUREFIRE WAYS TO KEEP THEM READING ALL YEAR!

BY AVA DRUTMAN AND DIANE HOUSTON

SCHOLASTIC
PROFESSIONAL BOOKS

New York • Toronto • London • Auckland • Sydney

•
_____

Dedicated
to our loving families—

Bob, Tara, and
Thomas Houston;
Lowell, Lee,
Scott, and Mark Drutman.

Thank you for your support
and enthusiasm.

_____
•

Scholastic Inc. grants teachers permission to photocopy the
activity sheets from this book for classroom use. No other part of
this publication may be reproduced in whole or in part, or stored
in a retrieval system, or transmitted in any form or by any means,
electronic, mechanical, photocopying, recording, or otherwise,
without written permission of the publisher. For information
regarding permission, write to Scholastic Inc., 730 Broadway,
New York, NY 10003.

Designed by Nancy Metcalf
Production by Intergraphics
Cover design by Anna V. Walker
Cover photograph by Jeff Heiges
Illustrations by Judy Nostrant, Stephanie Pershing

ISBN 0-590-49142-3

Keep Your Class Reading

PLACES AND SPACES FOR BOOKS

An Archaeological Dig

Use this idea to help pupils think about books they have read that others might like. "Imagine it's the year 2400. Archaeologists are searching through our school to learn more about children in the year _____ (current year). Someone discovers a box marked Class of _____'s Favorite Books. Which books will they find?"

Have children brainstorm the books that might be found in this box. Create a list of these titles. Then take out a large brown box that is marked "Class of _____'s Favorite Books." Over the next few days, help children fill the box with the suggested titles. They can come from the library, other classrooms, or homes. Encourage children to read those books they haven't read before. If time permits, have children write a note to the archaeologists telling why a particular book is his or her favorite.

Recommended Reading Table

At the beginning of the year, set up a Recommended Reading Table. Invite children to place a book that they recommend on the table. Have them write their name on a card and place it in or next to their book. As pupils choose one of these books, encourage them to ask questions of the person who recommended it to help them decide if the book is right for them.

A Suitcase of Titles

Someone can't seem to find a book that interests him or her? Just open a small suitcase that sits in the front of the room. It's filled with book titles written on index cards. On

CONTENTS

INTRODUCTION

Reading is a lifelong activity. As elementary school teachers we can establish a love for reading at an early age. Once deeply embedded, this love will remain part of our students' daily lives. This book is an attempt to help teachers meet their greatest challenge—to arouse a desire in children to read and foster the habit of reading. As teachers we can whet their appetites for books, develop an appreciation for all the elements of a book, and make reading exciting and stimulating. We can do this by keeping our approach to reading energized and vigorous. The purpose of this book is to provide teachers with vehicles to promote reading and reading-related activities every day, all year long.

In the past, after reading a book, children were always required to do a book report. Somehow the focus shifted from enjoying a book to writing a report. The goal of *150 Surefire Ways To Keep Them Reading All Year* is very different. It is to help children associate joy and pleasure with reading. The activities are designed to help children look at books in ways they haven't before. This book will give children ways to share their love of a book with their classmates, their school, and their community.

the back of the cards is a short blurb about the book and a place for children's comments. Children browse through the cards looking for a book that sounds interesting. Once they have read it, they add their comments to the card.

Heirloom Books

Some children may have personal books that were special to them at various stages of their lives. Help them preserve these precious feelings by creating Heirloom Boxes in which to store books they love. Ask pupils to bring cardboard boxes large enough to hold full-sized picture books. They decorate these containers, label them, and add their name. Suggest they keep the box in a special place at home, and look through it now and then. As they get older, the books will bring back fond memories of childhood.

A Sharing Box for Books and More

Get ready for a new unit of study in your classroom with a Sharing Box. Label the box with the title of the unit and ask students to help you fill it. Nonfiction books, magazine and newspaper articles, and stories about the topic are appropriate. Watch the box fill. As children add their contributions, interest in the new unit will accelerate. By the time the unit actually begins, you will be surprised by how much reading your students have already done.

Pockets for Recommended Reading

"What have you read that others might enjoy reading too?" Pupils can recommend books to others with this pocket graph. Set up a large piece of tag-board and write everyone's name down the left side of the board. Be sure to include your own name. Next to each name put a row of three pockets horizontally across the graph. They can be made of felt or tag-board

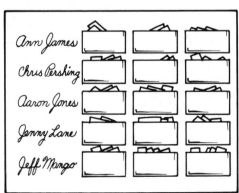

pieces and attached with glue or tape. Cut small pieces of oak tag to fit in the pockets.

As someone completes a book, he or she can decide if classmates would enjoy it. If the answer is yes, the pupil writes the title and author on an oak-tag slip and puts it into a pocket next to his or her name. Suggest children look at the cards others have in their pockets. They may wish to discuss a title with the child who has read it.

Outer Space Odyssey and More

Most children would like to travel to outer space, into the future, back in time, or to another land. Give them that chance with books and appliance boxes. Take outer space, for example. Over a period of a month, suggest pupils collect reading material about outer space. They can look for books, magazine and newspaper articles, or stories that they have written about outer space. While the reading material is stockpiling, they create a rocket ship from a large cardboard appliance box. Provide a variety of artistic media and let their imaginations go wild. Soon they will have a vehicle ready to travel to the farthest galaxy. Attach a banner that says "Reading is Out of This World." The reading materials, as well as one or two space seats, are placed inside the spaceship. Watch children travel to another planet, as they read in their rocket ship.

Appliance boxes can be turned into all sorts of other thematic places to read. They provide an atmosphere that heightens students' reading experiences. How about a teepee for pupils to travel back in time to when Native North Americans made their homes across the plains? It can be home for all kinds of reading material related to Native North Americans. (See the bibliography on page 61.) Or create a large boat, filled with reading material about sailboats, submarines, and yachts. Let students choose their own theme for an "appliance box." You may be surprised at their special interests.

NOTE: Before constructing a rocket ship, teepee, or boat check to make sure that this type of structure is not considered a fire hazard in your school.

Clever Book Containers

Pupils like to find books in all sorts of different containers. Fill unusual containers with books to delight your students. You can collect them from all sorts of places—home, kindergarten room, storage closet, yard sales, pupils' homes. How about placing books about trucks in an actual toy truck? Why not fill a huge pot or bowl with cookbooks? An empty animal cage filled with books about pets will amuse children. Children will happily browse through a large picnic basket holding favorite titles. Other containers are milk boxes, a baby bassinet, orange crate, suitcase, lunchbox, etc.

If you don't have unusual containers, display books in unusual places, such as:

○ windowsills
○ an easel
○ chalk tray in front of the chalkboard
○ clothesline strung tightly across a wall
○ a music stand
○ laid out on a carpet
○ a book mobile

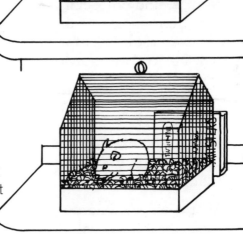

A Book Hunt

Why not hide books all around your classroom? Place them in ordinary and unusual spots. They can be found hiding in a desk or in a lunch bag. Invite children to hunt for the books. Watch them giggle as they discover the hiding places.

The Story Box

An element of surprise and curiosity keeps students motivated to read. A simple trunk or box filled with a book and some props will set the scene.

Select a book of short stories, fables, myths, legends, or folktales to place in the trunk. Besides the book, place some simple props

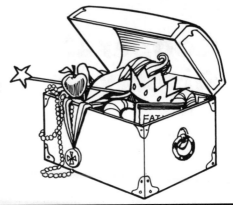

and costumes that could lend themselves to the story. Invite small groups of children to read one of the stories, then work cooperatively to create a short dramatization of it. Or, they might pull out the props before looking at the book and predict what the story will be about. They must read the story to see if their predictions are correct.

Change the book regularly and pupils will clamor to be the next ones to open the Story Box.

A Satchel of Books

Mary Poppins delights children whenever they encounter her. Why not bring a little bit of Mary Poppins to your classroom by finding or simulating a satchel similar to hers? (You can "create" it from a cardboard box and brown wrapping paper.) Place it beside your desk and fill it with books. They can be fiction or nonfiction, hardcover or paperback. Start each week by passing out books from your satchel. Children will anxiously anticipate which books will appear from your bag. If time permits, find a special book for each child. You might base your choice on their favorite author or type of book. Children really feel honored when they know you have considered their individual reading preferences.

Leave the "satchel" visible during the week. Children can then deposit the book in it when they have finished reading. They can also exchange it for a new one on their own. At the end of the week, put all the books back in the satchel. Each week intrigue your students with a satchel full of new books.

After a while, children may volunteer to select some of the books for the satchel. However your satchel gets filled, the end result is the same. Students will have a heightened interest in the books.

Cooperative Book Display Committees

Children enjoy having classroom responsibilities. Select a committee of four to six pupils to organize and set up a biweekly book display on a shelf or table. Ask them to choose a theme for their display. All the books might be

by the same author or about the same topic. Provide the group with time to carefully plan and select books. To enhance the display, children might bring in items that relate to the books. They might choose to create accompanying artwork. Ideally the members of the committee should be familiar with each book in the display so that if other children have questions about the books, they can be answered.

PLACES AND TIMES TO READ

Reading in Comfort

Having a cozy reading corner in your classroom promotes reading. All you need is a little space and a beanbag chair or two. Give children the opportunity to take a book and curl up in the corner. With younger students, a few stuffed animals will provide "friends" with whom to share a book.

Unusual Reading Spots

Children usually read sitting in their chairs at school. Once in a while add a touch of the unusual and let them choose their own reading spot. Perhaps someone has always wanted to sit under his or her desk. Maybe someone else has wanted to pick a corner, or lean up against the wall. Some, of course, may be quite content sitting in their seats. Just announce that it's time to grab a book, pick a spot, and read.

Read-Aloud Luncheons

Lunching and reading with the teacher is a great motivator. Invite children to bring lunch and a poem, joke, or riddle to share as all of you read aloud, discuss, giggle, and have fun together. Items must be brief and in good taste. Otherwise, the sky's the limit. Be sure you bring something to share too.

AWARENESS OF BOOKS AND THEIR SPECIAL PARTS

SPECIAL KINDS OF BOOKS

Remembering Your Babyhood with Books

Talk about books you enjoyed as a baby. Invite students who wish to share any similar experiences they may have had. If possible, display several of these books, particularly those designed for very young children. Discuss some of their features: very few words; sturdy construction; heavy paper, cardboard, or cloth pages; colorful but simple pictures. Then talk about the characteristics of young children to help pupils conclude why these books are made as they are.

A Delightfully Different Kind of Book Display

Create an awareness that books can come in different sizes and formats. There are pop-up books, picture books, scratch and sniff books, wordless books, and different shape books, just to name a few. There are big books and tiny books. There are books that have no illustrations. There are others that have no words. With your librarian, collect as many of these books as you can. Encourage children to bring any they might have at home. As a group, describe their designs; compare and contrast them. Discuss whether or not their uniqueness is an incentive for reading them or if it interferes with the books' stories. Do not expect total agreement on this point.

Flip, Turn, Pull, Unfold, Pop-Up

Manipulative books spark children's curiosity and invite the reader to interact with the book itself. Young children especially are excited to see what will flip open or pop out as they pull a tab or unfold a page. Set up a table with an assortment of these special books. The variety is amazing, from cut-out shapes to ones that may be tied together to form an object like a carousel. Remind children, however, that they must handle these books with extra care.

Here are a few of the authors who delight us with their unique books.

Janet and Allan Ahlberg
Eric Carle
Seymour Chwast
Robert Crowther
John S. Goodall
Tana Hoban
Ray Marshall

Lothar Meggendorfer
Bruno Munari
Ingrid Selberg
Annette Tison
Ron Van de Meer
A. & M. Provensen

Once pupils have read and manipulated some of these special books, challenge them to create their own manipulative books.

Old Books, New Books

Examining old books and other reading materials will give pupils clues to the interests, activities, homes, fashions, and ideas of readers a generation or more ago. Create a display of old books in your classroom. Parents, grandparents, and your local library may be able to share some. Search your school's storage rooms for old textbooks and readers. Have children look at the bindings, the print, the paper, and especially the illustrations. Invite them to compare and contrast them with books of today. In what ways are they alike? How are they different? Which ones seem most inviting to read?

There are some books whose stories are timeless. They have been printed in different versions and editions many times. If you can, find several editions of some of these classics, then compare and contrast them.

Alice in Wonderland
Bambi
Black Beauty
Call It Courage
Peter Pan
The Jungle Book

Hans Brinker or the Silver Skates
Heidi
The Secret Garden
The Wind in the Willows
Winnie the Pooh

Continue this comparison between the old and new. Collect old newspapers and magazines. If possible bring in a current and an old version of the same magazine. The articles and advertisements will provide important clues to the happenings and way of life of the day. Help pupils conclude how books explain and reflect current lifestyles. Can they predict what their children or grandchildren will say about the materials they are reading today?

Nonfiction Fling

To help children begin to appreciate nonfiction books, fill the room with books related to a topic you are studying. If you are studying the solar system, for example, divide the class into small groups. Invite each group to choose one of the planets. Then ask each pupil in that group to find a nonfiction book or article about that planet. Cooperative learning will take place as they read, discuss, and share thoughts about the information they have learned. Encourage children to pass along facts about other planets to other groups. Watch the excitement about reading nonfiction books fill your room.

Career Day

All children have dreams about what they hope to be when they grow up. Have children jot down the career of their dreams, then set up a career book table with at least one book to match each career mentioned. Once books have been read, plan a Career Day, when pupils come to school wearing or carrying something that represents the careers of their dreams.

Poetry Plus

Try this simple strategy for involving children in poetry. Set aside special times for children to read and listen to poetry. Make a good selection of poetry books available. Play recordings of poetry readings. Have children choose partners and a poem, find a quiet corner, and read the poem with their partners. Reading the poem aloud in a quiet voice will help them feel the rhythm and rhyme.

Encourage the children to respond physically to the rhythm as they read. They might interpret the rhythm with the swaying of their bodies or the stamping of their feet. As children develop a familiarity with poetry, they will choose to read it more often.

The Magic in Books

Help children enjoy the world of fantasy by imagining how objects are used in this type of literature. Prior to reading a fantasy story, bring in several items that are important to the story. Spark interest by discussing how these things might have magical uses. Then read the book aloud. Discuss students' predictions to see if they were correct.

For example: an umbrella, a ring, a wooden spoon, and a coin are important items in the fantasy books by Ruth Chew. Here are some of the titles in which these items are found:

The Trouble with Magic   *The Witch and the Ring*
The Witch at the Window   *Mostly Magic*
The Magic Coin   *What the Witch Left*

As children read other fantasy books, encourage them to bring them to the classroom along with the objects that have magical uses in the books. Challenge others to guess how they were used. Then encourage other children to find these books in the library and read them to discover the magic.

Wordless Books

Pictures tell the story in wordless books. Children are fascinated by this type of book. Gather these books from the library.

Here is a list of some authors who create wordless books:

Mitsumasa Anno   Peter Spier
Frank Asch   Hanne Turk
Alexandra Day   Iela Mari
John Goodall   Mercer Mayer
Tana Hoban   Jan Ormerod
Fernando Krahn

Fill your classroom with wordless books. Your students will naturally make up the story line to go with the pictures. Increase the enjoyment by inviting children to create their own wordless books. Have them work with a partner or in small groups. Set aside time for children to plan their books, and to try a variety of media such as pencil sketches, pen and ink, watercolor, markers, or crayons.

Once books are done, pupils exchange them and listen as others verbalize the story their books tell.

Creating Original Alphabet Books

Create a display of alphabet books. They can be found in every size, shape, and style. Some books use rhymes. Others make you laugh. Let the children pour over the alphabet books in all their different formats.

Once children have developed a familiarity with these, students will have a fantastic time developing their own alphabet books.

In the lower grades, creating these books develops a greater awareness of each letter. In the upper grades, the books are a creative experience that can be shared with younger children. You might ask the school librarian to create a special table for alphabet books in the library and to save a place for those your group has created.

OTHER READING MATERIALS

The Reading Box

Excite children by saying, "Will next week be the week for reading mysteries or cereal boxes? The question will be answered after the secret card is drawn."

With the Reading Box, students will be exposed to all types of reading material. Fill a box with cards that name things to read, including the somewhat unusual. One card for each of the following could be in your box: mystery,

humor, jokes and riddles, pop-up book, fables, fairy tale, poem, nonfiction, historical fiction, biography, wordless book, novel, play, magazine article, news article, cereal box, label, travel brochure, comics, TV guide, newspaper movie section, etc. Let children add cards to your box as they discover other kinds of reading material. Each Friday, invite a volunteer to choose a card from your box without looking. Then, with the children, begin to collect that kind of reading material for the next week. Set up a table of those materials and set aside time each day for reading them. The Reading Box will make pupils more aware of the innumerable things to read.

Read-a-Day Calendar

Reading is part of living. Use the Read-a-Day Calendar on page 18 to create an awareness of the place of reading in our daily lives. These reading ideas will motivate children to read all kinds of printed material. Adjust activities to fit the interests and lives of your pupils. Urban children can find and read street signs or store window labels. Farm children can be asked to read livestock feed labels or farm machinery maintenance manuals. The calendar will heighten pupil awareness of the many different places where words appear in the world around us. Invite students to come up with additional reading activities for next month's calendar.

Magazine Mania Minutes

There are a multitude of magazines published on an amazing variety of subjects. Yet many children are unaware that there are magazines written just for them. Help them become aware of the wide assortment of children's magazines. Check out some popular magazines from the library and set them up on a table or rack in your classroom. Once a week have a Magazine Mania Minutes session of 15 or 20 minutes. (Make sure there's at least one magazine per pupil.) Some popular titles are given on page 19.

Read-a-Day Calendar

SUNDAY	MONDAY	TUESDAY	WEDNESDAY	THURSDAY	FRIDAY	SATURDAY
1 Read all the events on a calendar today.	**2** Make a bookmark today.	**3** Share a book with your sister or brother today.	**4** Read a chapter of a book to your mom or dad today.	**5** Listen to one of your friends read today.	**6** Read a graph today.	**7** Read the newspaper headlines today.
8 Read the comics today.	**9** Read a map today.	**10** Read a joke to your teacher today.	**11** Read during part of recess today.	**12** Read the back of a cereal box today.	**13** Read a soup can label today.	**14** Read a set of game instructions today.
15 Read five street signs today.	**16** Read a word definition in a dictionary today.	**17** Find someone's phone number and address in a telephone book today.	**18** Read a recipe in one of your mom's cookbooks today.	**19** Read the instructions for a computer program today.	**20** Read the TV program listing for today's programs.	**21** Read a travel pamphlet today.
22 Read a science magazine today.	**23** Read a poem today.	**24** Read a catalog today.	**25** Read the summary on the back of a video today.	**26** Read something that came in the mail today.	**27** Read to one of your friends today.	**28** Read a chart today.
29 Read the weather forecast in the newspaper today.	**30** Read five signs on store windows today.	**31** Read a magazine today.				

Magazine Titles

Younger Readers (K–2)

Children's Playmate

Highlights

Humpty Dumpty

Jack and Jill

Kid City

Owl—The Discovery Magazine for Children

Your Big Backyard (science)

Older Readers (3–6)

Children's Digest

Cobblestone—The History Magazine for Young People

Cricket

Dynamite

Faces—The Magazine about People

National Geographic World (science)

Ranger Rick (science)

Scienceland

Sports Illustrated for Kids

Stone Soup—The Magazine by Children

Zillions—Consumer Report for Kids

Zoonooz (animals)

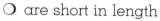

Book Blurbs

"Book Blurbs, Book Blurbs, Book Blurbs." Children repeating that tongue twister will fill your room with laughter. After the laughter subsides, pass out an assortment of books that have book blurbs on their front or back covers or jackets. Direct student attention to them and ask volunteers to read their blurbs aloud. What are blurbs designed to do? Help children conclude that a blurb is a positive statement designed to interest the reader in the book. Then challenge pupils to create their own blurbs for a book they are currently reading. Remind them that blurbs:

○ are short in length
○ make the reader want to read the entire book
○ never tell the whole story or how the plot's problem was solved.

Read Book Reviews

New books for children are being published all the time. How do we determine if the book is worthwhile? Sometimes we read it, but other times we count on book reviews. Why not let your students find out about a book by reading a book review written for children?

Scout out magazines that carry reviews of children's books: *Children's Digest* and *Stone Soup*. Select titles from the book reviews appropriate for your grade level and borrow them from your library. Use the reviews and the book in several ways:

1. Give children the reviews to read. Ask them to decide if they want to read the book on the basis of the review.
2. Have children read the book. Then have them read the review and decide whether or not they agree with the review.
3. Have children read a new book and write a review of it. Then have them read the published one and compare it with their own.

4. Have groups of pupils read the same books and reviews. Then have a discussion to compare group members' responses to the reviews and books.

Pupils can complete a related writing project. Have them write book reviews of favorite books, then bind the reviews together to make a class book reviews portfolio. Place it in the library. Let the entire school use your collected book reviews as a reference. Children like to read reviews written by their peers.

Don't Judge a Book by Its Cover

A book's cover is designed to "hook the reader" into reading a book. Sometimes the cover design matches the quality of the story. Other times it doesn't. Ask pupils if a book they chose by its cover lived up to its expectation. Have them tell about it. Collect several books pupils have read and look at their covers together. Discuss each one's merits. Could it be improved? How would you improve it? Then invite children to work with a partner to create a new and improved book cover for the book. Challenge them to create a cover that conveys to the reader what this book is about. Then display the newly created cover with the actual book cover. Invite other students to contrast and compare them.

Children may also have ideas for their own books. Why not follow up this activity with the creation of book covers for their own book?

While an attractive cover is often an incentive for selecting a book, help pupils develop other criteria for choosing a book, such as:

○ Read the book blurb to give you a feeling about the book.
○ Choose a topic you enjoy reading about.
○ Read a page or two to see if you think you will be able to read it easily.
○ Look for books by an author you have read before.
○ Ask a librarian for help.
○ Ask a friend who has read the book.

Finding a Title Page

The title page provides an assortment of information, but often it is overlooked. Ask pupils to choose a book and find the title page. Have them identify the different information in the page. Who is the author? The illustrator? The publisher? As children identify them, they might form into groups with the same author or publisher.

Then have pupils turn the page to see if there is a copyright date. Explain that this date tells when the book was first published so readers can tell when the book was written. This would be important to know when reading a nonfiction book.

This Is Dedicated to . . .

Some books have dedication pages. Although these pages are very special to the author, they are often unnoticed by the reader. With the class answer and discuss these questions:

○ What is a dedication?
○ Why might an author dedicate a book to someone or more than one person?
○ What does *dedicate* mean?

Then examine dedications in several books most pupils have read. What theories can children come up with about the reason for these dedications? Encourage children to dedicate their own classmade books to someone—a friend, a family member, a pet, a teacher, and so on.

Dedicated to my dog SPUNKY. Thanks for being my friend.

School Words Scavenger Hunt

Reinforce the importance of reading with a scavenger word hunt through your school. Appoint a recorder who has a clipboard, paper, and pencil. Then walk through the halls and into special rooms or playground areas. Pause whenever a word is discovered and ask the recorder to write the word. Discuss with children the different ways that words are used: to inform, to identify, or to express ideas. How many words are discovered on the hunt? Post the list in the classroom for children to add to as they visit other parts of the school.

Books Are Made of Paper

When we read, we are concerned about the words and illustrations. But how often do we notice the paper? Set up a display of books that have different kinds of paper. Talk about why certain kinds of paper are used for certain kinds of books. For example, baby books have very heavy paper, cardboard, or even cloth pages to withstand rough usage. Art books usually have heavy, glossy finish paper so the illustrations will reproduce better. Books that will be used very frequently, such as textbooks, have paper that is tough and resists ripping. Encourage pupils to think about whether the paper makes a difference in their enjoyment of the book.

Ask pupils to think about the paper when they make their own personal books. Would using a special color add to its appeal? Would using varying kinds of paper add or detract from the plot of the story? Thinking about these ideas will make pupils more aware of the place of paper in designing a book.

The Printed Word Up Close

Pupils will find it fun to compare the sizes and kinds of type used in books and other reading materials. Collect a variety of materials using different kinds and sizes. Find materials that use bold and italic as well as regular roman type. As pupils look at them, discuss why some words are bold, others italic. A play, for example, usually puts stage directions in italic and actors' speeches in roman. The actors' names might be in bold or in capital letters. Discuss how this use of different types makes it easier to read the play.

Talk about some of the decorative types, especially those used for titles or for labels in picture books. Why were they used? What special effects do they give? The group might make a classroom collage of interesting types cut from newspapers, magazines, advertising brochures, and so on. Then give pupils a chance to design their own decorative types.

Calling All Types of Book Bindings

The way the pages of a book are put together is called a binding. Some books have their pages sewn or stapled in a form called saddle stitching; others are perfect bound with sections glued together; still others have wire or plastic coils that create a spiral-bound book. Collect books with different kinds of bindings and leave them on the reading table for a few days so everyone has a chance to examine them in free time. After several days, talk about why the publisher might have used each kind of binding and the advantages of each. A pupil who seems most interested in this topic might read about book binding in an encyclopedia and then offer to give a demonstration of the steps in binding a book.

Admiring the Art

Illustrations are an important part of many books. Collect several books that have interesting illustrations. Include as many different styles as possible. Put them on the reading table and have pupils look at them in free time. After several days, select two or three books and discuss each one's illustrations, using these questions:

○ What medium does the artist use? (The medium is generally printed on the copyright page.)
○ Is the artwork fanciful or realistic?
○ Are the drawings traditional or avant-garde?
○ What kinds of designs are used on the pages?
○ Are the colors bold or soft?
○ Are the lines definite or sketchy?
○ Are there a lot of details in the drawings?
○ How are the illustrations placed on the page?
○ If there are photographs, do they illustrate something or create a mood?
○ How do the illustrations make you feel?

Finally, have students vote on the book whose illustrations appeal to them most. Hopefully each book will have several votes, so pupils will realize that tastes differ and that diversity in tastes is what makes each of us unique. For further focus on the illustrations in books, see "Illustrators I Love" on page 27, "Which Books Are Caldecott Medal Winners?" on page 27, and "Imagination vs. Illustration" on page 28.

Borders in Books

Book illustrators use different ways to illustrate books. One way is to put a border around each page. A border unites a page and helps to tell the story. Let children use the bibliography on the next page to discover borders in books. Have pupils look closely at the borders to find small details, then read to see how these details illustrate the story. The next time pupils write a story, suggest they illustrate it with a border.

End Pages

Open a book! Close a book! Attractive end pages lead you out of a story. Help children develop an awareness of the significance of artistic end pages in a book. Have children look at the end pages of several books. Some are plain, others colored, and some cleverly designed. The illustrator may use an end page to set a mood, introduce characters, give clues to the plot, or provide a map that is important to the story. Invite children to compare and contrast several books' end pages. Remind them to look at end pages when starting a new book. Then challenge them to create end pages for one of their favorite titles.

Books with Borders Bibliography

Bowdan, Joan Chase, *Why the Tides Ebb and Flow*, ill. Marc Brown (Houghton Mifflin, 1979)

Brett, Jan, *Annie and the Wild Animals* (Houghton Mifflin, 1985)

Brett, Jan, *The First Dog* (Harcourt Brace Jovanovich, 1988)

Brett, Jan, retold & ill., *Goldilocks and the Three Bears* (Dodd, Mead, & Co., 1987)

Brett, Jan, adapt. & ill., *The Mitten* (G. P. Putnam's Sons, 1989)

Brett, Jan, *The Wild Christmas Reindeer* (G. P. Putnam's Sons, 1990)

dePaola, Tomie, retold & ill., *Fin M'Coul, The Giant of Knockmany Hill* (Holiday, 1981)

dePaola, Tomie, *The Hunter and the Animals* (Holiday, 1981)

Esbensen, Barbara Juster, *The Star Maiden*, ill. Helen K. Davie (Little, Brown, & Co., 1988)

Hague, Michael, ill., *Cinderella and Other Tales from Perrault* (Holt, 1989)

Hodges, Margaret, retold, *Saint George and the Dragon*, ill. Trina Schart Hyman (Little, Brown, & Co., 1984)

Hyman, Trina Schart, retold & ill., *Little Red Riding Hood* (Holiday, 1983)

LeCain, Errol, retold & ill., *The Twelve Dancing Princesses* (Viking, 1978)

McVitty, Walter, retold, *Ali Baba and the Forty Thieves*, ill. Margaret Early (Harry N. Abrams, Inc., 1989)

Ormerod, Jan, retold & ill., *The Frog Prince* (Lothrop, Lee, & Shepard, 1990)

Stanley, Diane, *Fortune* (Morrow Jr. Books, 1990)

AUTHORS AND ILLUSTRATORS

Illustrators I Love

Display an assortment of beautifully illustrated books. Hold up two with quite different illustrations and ask the children to contrast and compare them. What do they like in each illustration? What does not appeal to them? Lead the discussion in the following directions:

○ Which are more enjoyable, black and white illustrations or color ones?
○ Do you prefer illustrations that inform or that set a mood?
○ Do the illustrations help you to read the words? If yes, how?
○ Do the illustrations tell you information that is not written? If yes, how?

Begin a favorite illustrators' chart. Over a period of time pupils can notice and discuss illustrations they like, check the name of the illustrator from the title or copyright page, and write his or her name on the chart. Later they can have an Illustrator of the Week Celebration where several books by an illustrator are displayed and shared.

Which Books Are Caldecott Medal Winners?

A magnificently illustrated book is a treasure to behold. The Caldecott Award is given each year to the illustrator of the most distinguished American picture book for children published during the preceding year. The first award was made in 1938. The artwork in Caldecott Medal winners is never short of magnificent. Sharing these books with your students will definitely focus their attention on illustrators and their illustrations. Collect several of these Caldecott Award books and display them on a special table. Invite children to scout them out themselves. The medal sticker on the front of the book will signal that they have met a winner.

Have pupils become "judges" for a Caldecott Award. Give them time to look at the books you collected for the previous activity and evaluate each for the award by answering the following questions:

○ Is the style appropriate for the text?
○ Is the medium appropriate for the text? (The medium used is generally printed on the copyright page.)
○ Do the illustrations and text go together well, and not compete with each other?
○ Would the illustrations appeal to most children?
○ What makes the illustrations unique, out of the ordinary?

After a lively discussion, vote on which book the class would have picked as the winner.

Imagination vs. Illustration

While illustrations usually add to a reader's appreciation of a book, sometimes an illustration can hamper the imagination. Read aloud a very descriptive section of an unfamiliar illustrated book or an entire book. Ask children to close their eyes and visualize what is being read. Hopefully they will see it as clearly as the author did when the words were written. Then ask them to describe what they saw. After all have shared their visualization, show the book's illustration. Let children think about which they enjoyed viewing more . . . their visualization or the illustration. An ideal choice for this read-aloud experiment is *Two Bad Ants* by Chris Van Allsburg.

Authors Are People Too!

Calling everyone's favorite authors! Most pupils will have not paid much attention to the names of the persons who wrote the books they have read. Take them to the library and let them browse through the books. Help them to recall which books they have read and to notice their authors. Within a period of time, all pupils should be able to choose an author they enjoy reading.

Help children be curious about these authors. Brainstorm questions they might have about an author. Duplicate the list, give a copy to each pupil, and send them out to find answers. Here are some of the ways they can find their answers.

O Reading book jackets that have biographical information about the author.
O Writing to the author. (Please let children know that they do not always write back.)
O Reading the portion about their favorite author in the reference books, *Something About the Author, Meet the Authors and Illustrators,* and *Books Are by People.*

Author Day

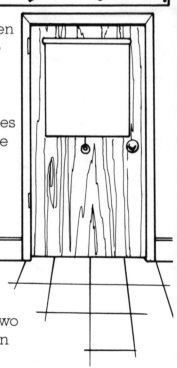

What if Ezra Jack Keats met H. A. Rey? This could happen on Author Day in your classroom. Have a day when the children pretend they are famous authors. This activity works best if it is done in conjunction with "Authors Are People Too!" Create a banner that says Author Day to hang over your doorway. Give each "author" five minutes to talk about the joys and problems of writing. Challenge your students by asking them some of the following questions. By using a combination of information and imagination, students can respond.

O How do you feel about your books?
O What it was like to write a book?
O Describe any difficulties you had writing.
O Which book is your favorite? Why?
O Which character do you like the least in your books?

This activity might be more effective in your classroom if two pupils a week were "authors" and talked to each other in front of the class about their lives and their writings.

Favorite Authors Bulletin Board

Do the pupils in your class read the same authors continually? (This may change over the course of the school year.) Create a bulletin board for three popular ones. List each author across the top of the board. Then invite children to put up information about that author under the name. Children can put up book covers of his or her books, their responses to his or her books, or articles about the author. Change the board every week or so to call attention to other authors.

Read a Newbery Award Winner

The first Newbery Award was given in 1922. This award is given to the author of the most distinguished contribution to American literature for children published the preceding year. Only one each year is chosen for the Newbery Award. Help children to recognize these books by pointing out the gold medal that the Newbery Award winner receives.

Encourage children to read one or more Newbery Award winners. If several children have read the same book, encourage them to discuss why they believe the book was chosen. Invite them to think about the following:

○ The author's style
○ How the setting enhances the book
○ How the plot is developed
○ How the characters develop
○ The theme of the book
○ The genre of the book

Children will no doubt become involved with evaluating the worth of this Newbery Award winner. They may or may not agree with the judges' decision.

Name That Title and Author Game

Here's a new twist on an old familiar game that will activate students' critical thinking skills.

1. Think of an author whose books you have read in class.
2. Have children ask you questions about the books—the characters, setting, style of writing, or plot—in order to guess the author.
3. Give only "yes" and "no" answers.

Students will be reminded of facts about the books and authors as they play.

Once children are familiar with this game, divide the class into teams. Each team selects a book or story that has been read in class and the same questioning methods are used. Each team's goal is to guess the title and author of the book in the fewest number of questions. The number of questions equals the number of points given. Twenty-five questions is the maximum number of questions that can be asked.

CREATORS' BIRTHDAYS

Happy Birthday, Authors and Illustrators

Children will enjoy knowing when authors and illustrators celebrate their birthdays. Use the "Authors and Illustrators Birthday Calendar" found on pages 33–44. This calendar highlights author and illustrator birthdays month by month. Transfer the dates onto the current year's calendar and display it in a special location in your classroom. Hang a banner that says "Happy Birthday, Authors and Illustrators."

Celebrate Authors' Birthdays

Surprise an author by sending a poster-size birthday card from your class. Each month have your students choose an author they are familiar with from the "Authors and Illustrators Birthday Calendar" found on pages 33–44. During that month, encourage your students to read one or more books by that author.

Then have them draw a picture of their favorite book, book character, or scene from the book on the card and sign their name.

NOTE: Send the card to the writer's publisher, who will forward it to the writer.

In addition, why not have a birthday party for that author on his or her birthday? At the party, display books written by that author and talk about the books pupils have read. At the end of the party, vote to determine the class's favorite book written by that author.

Author Birthday Match-Up

"Guess which author has the same birthday as you?" Match up the children in your class with authors and illustrators who share the same birthday. Use the "Authors and Illustrators Birthday Calendar" found on pages 33–44. Encourage children to read at least one book by that author during the month of their birthday. Here are some additional connections you might want to make:

○ On the child's birthday, he or she can present a book talk about this book or the author.
○ Read aloud a book or a portion of a book by this author.
○ Give the children a book written by that author as a birthday gift.

January Authors and Illustrators

SUNDAY	MONDAY	TUESDAY	WEDNESDAY	THURSDAY	FRIDAY	SATURDAY
			1 Barbara Williams	**2** Isaac Asimov Crosby Bonsall	**3** Joan Walsh Anglund Carolyn Haywood J.R.R. Tolkien	**4** Jacob Grimm Fernando Krahn
5	**6** Carl Sandburg	**7** Kay Chorao Eleanor Clymer	**8** Lee J. Ames (Illustrator)	**9** Clyde Robert Bulla	**10**	**11**
12 Charles Perrault	**13** Michael Bond	**14**	**15**	**16**	**17** John Bellairs Robert Cormier	**18** Raymond Briggs A. A. Milne
19	**20**	**21**	**22** Brian Wildsmith Blair Lent	**23**	**24**	**25**
26 Harry Allard Lewis Carroll	**27**	**28** Rosemary Wells Bill Peet	**29** Lloyd Alexander Tony Johnston	**30** Gerald McDermott	**31**	

February Authors and Illustrators

SUNDAY	MONDAY	TUESDAY	WEDNESDAY	THURSDAY	FRIDAY	SATURDAY
						1
2 Judith Viorst Rebecca Caudill	**3**	**4** Russell Hoban	**5**	**6**	**7** Charles Dickens Laura Ingalls Wilder	**8** Anne Rockwell Adrienne Adams
9 Dick Gackenbach	**10** E. L. Konigsburg	**11** Jane Yolen	**12** Judy Blume	**13**	**14**	**15** Norman Bridwell Michael Thaler
16 Mary O'Neill	**17** Robert Newton Peck	**18**	**19** Louis Slobodkin Lee Harding	**20**	**21**	**22**
23	**24** Wilhelm Grimm	**25** Cynthia Voigt	**26**	**27** Florence Parry Heide Henry Wadsworth Longfellow	**28**	**29**

March Authors and Illustrators

SUNDAY	MONDAY	TUESDAY	WEDNESDAY	THURSDAY	FRIDAY	SATURDAY
1	**2** Dr. Seuss Leo Dillon (Illustrator)	**3**	**4**	**5** Mem Fox	**6** Thacher Hurd	**7**
8 Edna Miller Kenneth Grahame	**9**	**10**	**11** Wanda Gag Ezra Jack Keats	**12** Virginia Hamilton	**13** Diane Dillon (Illustrator)	**14**
15 Barbara Cohen	**16** Sid Fleischman	**17** Kate Greenaway (Illustrator)	**18**	**19**	**20** Lois Lowry Mitsumasa Anno Ellen Conford	**21** Phyllis McGinley Margaret Mahy
22 Randolph Caldecott (Illustrator) Harry Devlin	**23** Eleanor Cameron	**24**	**25**	**26** Robert Frost Betty MacDonald	**27**	**28**
29	**30** Charles Keller	**31**				

April Authors and Illustrators

SUNDAY	MONDAY	TUESDAY	WEDNESDAY	THURSDAY	FRIDAY	SATURDAY
			1 Jan Wahl	**2** Hans Christian Andersen	**3** Washington Irving	**4** Elizabeth Levy
5	**6**	**7** Tony Palazzo Donald Carrick	**8** Ruth Chew Trina Schart Hyman (Illustrator)	**9**	**10** David Adler	**11**
12 C. W. Anderson Beverly Cleary	**13** Lee Bennett Hopkins	**14**	**15** Eleanor Schick	**16** Gertrude Chandler Warner Garth Williams (Illustrator)	**17**	**18**
19	**20**	**21**	**22**	**23**	**24** Evaline Ness	**25** Alvin Schwartz
26 Patricia Reilly Giff	**27** Ludwig Bemelmens John Burningham	**28**	**29**	**30**		

May Authors and Illustrators

SUNDAY	MONDAY	TUESDAY	WEDNESDAY	THURSDAY	FRIDAY	SATURDAY
					1	**2**
3	**4** Don Wood (Illustrator)	**5** Leo Lionni	**6** Judy Delton	**7** Nonny Hogrogian	**8**	**9** James Barrie Eleanor Estes William Pene du Bois
10	**11** Sheila Burnford	**12** Edward Lear	**13**	**14** George Selden	**15** L. Frank Baum Ellen MacGregor	**16**
17	**18** Lillian Hoban	**19**	**20** Carol Carrick	**21**	**22** Arnold Lobel	**23** Scott O'Dell Peter Parnall Margaret Wise Brown Oliver Butterworth
24	**25** Martha Alexander Bennett Cerf	**26**	**27**	**28**	**29**	**30** Millicent Selsam
31 Jay Williams Elizabeth Coatsworth						

June Authors and Illustrators

SUNDAY	MONDAY	TUESDAY	WEDNESDAY	THURSDAY	FRIDAY	SATURDAY
	1 James Daugherty	**2** Paul Galdone (Illustrator)	**3** Anita Lobel	**4**	**5** Richard Scarry Franklin Branley	**6** Verna Aardema Cynthia Rylant Peter Spier
7 John Goodall (Illustrator)	**8**	**9**	**10** Maurice Sendak	**11**	**12** Johanna Spyri	**13**
14 Janice May Udry	**15**	**16**	**17** Beatrice Schenk DeRegniers	**18** Chris Van Allsburg Pat Hutchins	**19**	**20**
21 Robert Kraus	**22**	**23**	**24**	**25** Eric Carle	**26** Lynd Ward Nancy Willard Charlotte Zolotow	**27**
28 Esther Forbes	**29** Antoine de Saint Exupery	**30** David McPhail				

July Authors and Illustrators

SUNDAY	MONDAY	TUESDAY	WEDNESDAY	THURSDAY	FRIDAY	SATURDAY
			1	**2** Jean George	**3**	**4**
5	**6**	**7**	**8**	**9**	**10** Martin Provensen	**11** E. B. White
12	**13** Marcia Brown	**14** Peggy Parish	**15** Clement Moore Walter Edmonds	**16** Richard Egielski (Illustrator) Shirley Hughes	**17**	**18**
19 Eve Merriam	**20**	**21**	**22** Margery Williams	**23** Patricia Coombs Robert Quackenbush	**24**	**25**
26 Jan Berenstain	**27** Scott Corbett	**28** Natalie Babbitt Beatrix Potter	**29**	**30**	**31** Lynne Banks Reid	

39

August Authors and Illustrators

SUNDAY	MONDAY	TUESDAY	WEDNESDAY	THURSDAY	FRIDAY	SATURDAY
						1 Gail Gibbons
2 Holling C. Holling James Howe	**3** Mary Calhoun	**4**	**5** Robert Bright Ruth Sawyer	**6** Barbara Cooney Frank Asch	**7** Betsy Byars Maia Wojciechowska	**8** Trinka Hakes Noble
9 Jose Aruego (Illustrator)	**10**	**11** Don Freeman Steven Kroll Johanna Cole	**12** Deborah Howe	**13**	**14** Robert Crowe Alice Provensen	**15** Edith Nesbit Mark Taylor Brinton Turkle
16 Matt Christopher	**17** Myra Cohn Livingston Ariane Dewey Aruego (Illustrator)	**18** Louise Fatio	**19**	**20**	**21** Arthur Yorinks	**22**
23 Dick Bruna	**24**	**25**	**26** Bernard Wiseman	**27** Graham Oakley	**28** Phyllis Krasilovsky Roger Duvoisin Tasha Tudor	**29**
30 Laurent de Brunhoff Virginia Lee Burton Donald Crews	**31**					

September Authors and Illustrators

SUNDAY	MONDAY	TUESDAY	WEDNESDAY	THURSDAY	FRIDAY	SATURDAY
		1	**2** Bernard Most	**3** Aliki Brandenberg	**4** Syd Hoff Joan Aiken	**5**
6	**7** Elmer Hader	**8** Byron Barton Jack Prelutsky	**9** Aileen Fisher	**10**	**11**	**12**
13 Else Holmelund Minarik Roald Dahl	**14** Elizabeth Winthrop Edith Thacher Hurd John Steptoe Diane Goode (Illustrator)	**15** Watty Piper Tomie dePaola Robert McCloskey	**16** H. A. Rey	**17** Paul Goble	**18**	**19** Rachel Field
20	**21** Taro Yashima	**22**	**23**	**24** Wilson Rawls	**25**	**26**
27 Bernard Waber	**28**	**29** Stan Berenstain	**30** Edgar d'Aulaire Alvin Tresselt			

October Authors and Illustrators

SUNDAY	MONDAY	TUESDAY	WEDNESDAY	THURSDAY	FRIDAY	SATURDAY
				1 Louis Untermeyer	**2**	**3** John Carl Himmelman Molly Cone Natalie Savage Carlson
4 Robert Lawson Donald Sobol Munro Leaf	**5**	**6** Steven Kellogg	**7** Susan Jeffers (Illustrator) Alice Dalgliesh	**8** Edward Ormondroyd	**9** Johanna Hurwitz	**10** James Marshall
11	**12**	**13**	**14** Miriam Cohen	**15**	**16** Ronald Himler	**17**
18	**19** Ed Emberley (Illustrator)	**20** Crockett Johnson	**21**	**22**	**23** Marjorie Flack	**24** Bruno Munari
25	**26**	**27**	**28** Leonard Kessler	**29**	**30**	**31** Katherine Paterson

November Authors and Illustrators

SUNDAY	MONDAY	TUESDAY	WEDNESDAY	THURSDAY	FRIDAY	SATURDAY
1	**2** Margaret Bloy Graham	**3**	**4** Gail Haley	**5** Marcia Sewall	**6**	**7**
8 Marianna Mayer	**9**	**10**	**11**	**12** Marjorie Weiman Sharmat	**13** Nathaniel Benchley Robert Louis Stevenson	**14** Astrid Lindgren Miska Miles William Steig
15 Daniel Pinkwater	**16** Jean Fritz	**17**	**18**	**19** Margaret Musgrove	**20**	**21** Elizabeth George Speare Leo Politi
22	**23** Marc Simoni (Illustrator)	**24** Carlo Collodi	**25** Marc Brown	**26** Charles Schulz	**27**	**28** Stephanie Calmerson Tomi Ungerer
29 Louisa May Alcott C. S. Lewis	**30** Margot Zemach L. M. Montgomery Mark Twain					

❄ December Authors and Illustrators ❄

SUNDAY	MONDAY	TUESDAY	WEDNESDAY	THURSDAY	FRIDAY	SATURDAY
		1 Jan Brett	**2** David Macauley	**3**	**4**	**5** Harve Zemach
6 Elizabeth Yates	**7**	**8** Kin Platt James Thurber	**9** Jean de Brunhoff	**10** Barbara Emberley	**11**	**12**
13 Leonard Weisgard (Illustrator)	**14**	**15**	**16** Marie Hall Ets	**17**	**18** Marilyn Sachs	**19** Eve Bunting
20	**21**	**22**	**23** Rudyard Kipling	**24** John Langstaff	**25**	**26** Jean Van Leeuwen
27 Ingri d'Aulaire	**28**	**29**	**30** Mercer Mayer	**31**		

44

CELEBRATIONS, AWARDS, AND GAMES

CELEBRATIONS

Book Parties Galore

Book parties promote interest in reading and encourage informal activities based on books. There are a multitude of themes for book parties. Here are a few.

A Book Theme Party

Have a "Digging for Dinosaurs Party" or "Our Funniest Book Party." Fill your room with books that relate to that theme. During the party, children browse through the books, share comments about them, enjoy a game or contest based on the theme, and have a snack or make decorations related to it. For instance, at the dinosaur party, serve cookies cut out in the shape of dinosaurs; at "Our Funniest Book Party" provide place mats that have jokes and riddles on them to read and enjoy. Play such relay races as "Pass the Dinosaur Bone" or "Answer This Riddle."

Other theme ideas might be:

Ocean party
Pioneer party
Colonial party
Animals, Animals, Animals
 (or one specific one)
Space party

Dragons party
Fairy Tales and Fables party
Science Fiction party
Nursery Rhyme party
Sports party
Mystery book party

"Who Are You?" Party

Could you be Peter Pan? Are you the Hungry Caterpillar, eating everything in sight? Invite children to become a favorite book character. They wear simple costumes they create from grocery bags and behave as those characters would. On the day prior to the party, try to have children find a copy of the book in which they appear. Display all the books. At the party, everyone sits in a large circle as each, in turn, comes into the center and talks about his or her adventures in the book. Classmates try to guess who the book character is. The child who correctly identifies the character has the first chance to borrow the book from the display table to read. If possible, a few children might visit another classroom to see if those pupils can guess which characters your students are.

Historical Fiction Fête

One popular genre with older students is historical fiction. Have students read historical fiction books which take place in a particular century. After everyone has read at least one book, have a Century Sensation Party, based on the books they have read. Invite them to dress as a person from that century. Serve treats that would have been served at that time in history. Sing songs and do dances from that century. Learn and play games that children of that century would have played.

As a variation of this idea, plan a Dynamic Decade Party, focusing on a specific decade in history.

An Ethnic Experience

Through books pupils can learn about their own and other heritages. With the exception of Native Americans, everyone's ancestors came from another country. Have children list the country or countries from which their ancestors originated. They then go to the library to find nonfiction and fiction books about that country. Native Americans can read books about their tribal ancestry. Once reading is done, have them share the information at an ethnic party. Several children with the same origin can work together.

Sharing can take many forms:

○ A map of the country can be presented with the place of origin marked.
○ Drawings or photos of the country can be displayed.
○ Excerpts from letters from relatives or friends in the country can be read.

○ Newly arrived pupils might talk about their previous life, or a parent, grandparent, or older sibling might visit the class.

○ Books or magazines in the language of the country can be shared.

○ Songs, games, special foods, national costumes can be explained or shared.

This sharing of heritages is a good December activity. At this time of year there are many special holidays celebrated by a variety of ethnic groups. Even those groups that celebrate the same holiday often do it with different foods, games, songs, decorations, and so on. Make your holiday party a multiethnic book experience this year.

Read-Aloud Guests

Ask guests to come to read aloud in your classroom. Invite a parent, a grandparent, the principal, the superintendent, the nurse, another teacher, a member of your family, a political leader, or any other special personality. The children love the change of pace and a new voice. You could ask your guests to bring in one of their favorite books to read, but screen it first. Have children gather around your special guest and watch faces fill with delight as the story begins. Allow time after the reading for guest and pupils to socialize and talk about their reading interests.

Book Fan Clubs

Fan clubs for celebrity book characters generate an excitement about reading that is contagious. When those characters appear in a series, children have many opportunities to really learn about them.

Here are some popular series for younger readers:

○ the "Frog and Toad" books by Arnold Lobel
○ the "Arthur" books by Lillian Hoban
○ the "Frances" books by Russell Hoban
○ the "Amelia Bedelia" books by Peggy Parish
○ the "Cam Jansen" books by David Adler
○ the "Fourth Floor Twins" books by David Adler
○ the "Fox" books by Edward Marshall

○ the "George and Martha" books by James Marshall
○ the "Nate the Great" books by Marjorie Weinman Sharmat
○ the "Little Bear" books by Minarik
○ the "Clifford" books by Norman Bridwell
○ the "M & M" books by Pat Ross
○ the "The Kids of the Polk Street School" books by Patricia Reilly Giff

Here are some popular series for older readers:

○ the "Baby Sitters Club" books by Anne Martin
○ the "Encyclopedia Brown" Books by Donald L. Sobol
○ the "Betsy" and "Eddie" books by Carolyn Haywood
○ the "Henry," "Ellen," and "Ramona" books by Beverly Cleary
○ the "Little House" books by Laura Ingalls Wilder

Invite children to become members of the "Arthur" Fan Club or the "Ramona" Fan Club by reading books that they appear in. Create membership cards on which pupils list the books they have read. Have regular meetings when an incident from a book is read and enjoyed. Plan ways to interest others in the club. Posters that advertise a fan club are made and displayed. "Ramona" or "Arthur" tee-shirts can be made and worn on the day the fan club meets.

Celebrate and Appreciate New Books

New books are always special treats. When they arrive, celebrate! Talk about the bright and colorful protective book jackets, the crisp, clean new pages, and even the "new" smell. Carefully pass the books around. Let each child handle the books personally. Discuss how to care for books. Encourage children to treat them as they would a good friend. Read a chapter from one of them and use the "Pick a Name" box (page 51) to see who gets to take it home.

Joke Jamboree

Have a hilarious time in your classroom with a Joke Jamboree. Invite all your students to bring in their joke books. Start the day of the jamboree by telling a joke. Then have a joke time when students can tell jokes to one another from their own books or ones you've provided. During the day, also provide time for students to just sit down, read, and giggle.

End the jamboree with a snack of joke juice—fruit juice colored with food coloring to disguise its flavor until tasted.

Funniest Book

Tales of a Fourth Grade Nothing
Title
Judy Blume
Author

AWARDS

Create-a-Book Award

Creating their own awards is a great way for children to convey their feelings about books. This activity would be good to use after discussing the Caldecott and Newbery Awards (pages 27 and 30).

Best Dog Book

Spunky
Title
Dori Brink
Author

Individual awards can be given to any book by a student, but the criteria for choosing must be determined and written so others will understand the award.

Book awards can be given for such things as:

Best Illustrated Book   Best Thanksgiving Book
Most Entertaining Book   Best Dog Book Ever Written

Best Book with a Lesson

Yertle the Turtle
Title
Dr. Seuss
Author

Children may wish to create an award using their own name. For instance: The Betsy Award, The Mark Award, The Cooper Award.

What about giving an award for a book character? Is there a plot or a theme that is simply unforgettable? Let your students develop an eye for quality and then reward it.

Once the book is chosen, children can use the reproducible awards on page 50 as a starting point. With a little help from crayons and markers, they can create the award. A little glue, a bottle of glitter, and ribbons will allow your children to create some "award-winning" awards.

Best Illustrated Book

On Market Street
Title
Anita Lobel
Author

Title

Author

Title

Author

Title

Author

Title

Author

Post the awards on a Book Award Wall and display the books on a table beneath it. Awards will motivate other students to read these books. Don't be surprised if your classroom is filled with lively discussions about whether the book truly deserved an award.

The Class Book Award of the Month Goes to . . .

Individual awards are exciting, but what about creating Reading Group and Class Awards. These awards require children to work cooperatively to determine the criteria as well as the design of the awards. The criteria could be posted. Then children can refer to it when thinking about giving an award.

Here are some reasons for awards to which children can really relate:

○ The book we just couldn't put down!
○ The book that touched our feelings the most.
○ The book that EVERYONE would want to read.
○ The book that made us say, "We want to read another book just like this one!"

Each month have children work cooperatively to choose one book and give it an award. Plan a simple ceremony for presenting these coveted book awards. Announce, over the public address system, what book won the Class Award from your class. Be sure to tell the reason for the award. Let the librarian know which book was chosen before the announcement. Perhaps an extra copy or two can be borrowed to take care of the rush that is sure to come.

GAMES

Pick a Name

Nothing encourages interest in a book more than being the "winner" of it. Have each child write his or her name on a slip of paper. Write the words "Pick a Name" on a box with a hole the width of a hand in its top. Then place the slips of paper in the box.

Select a book that you know the children in your class will enjoy. Give a mini-book talk about it. Then display it in a place of honor in the room—on a table, on a music stand, or prominently placed on your desk. Tell the children that one of them will be able to borrow this book to take home to read. Reach into your box and pull out a name. If your class is reading picture books, draw a new name each day. If your students are reading longer books, have weekly drawings. Let the drawing take on a ceremonious flavor to help generate even more enthusiasm. An excitement toward books builds as the book pick continues.

Book Break

Create enthusiasm with the unexpected. Every so often, stop everything and hold up an attractive sign that says Book Break! Children will quickly learn that this means to stop doing their current activity. For about five minutes read an exciting portion from a book that is at a reading level appropriate for your class. Then show the book, read the title and author, and ask the magic question, "Who wants to read this book?" Make a list of interested children and post it. As each child on this list reads the book, he or she crosses off his or her name and gives the book to the next child on the list.

Enhance this idea by asking the librarian, the physical education teacher, the music teacher, the art teacher, the principal, or a parent to pop in with a Book Break. You may also want to prearrange with children to surprise the class with a Book Break.

Be That Character Charades

Playing a simple charade game is a good way to call attention to memorable book characters. Perhaps a character has a specific accent or walks in a special way. Invite children to imitate a character without telling anyone else who it is. Others try to guess who it is and explain how they knew it was that character. Always make sure the book from which that character came is available in the classroom or library so pupil interest in reading can be maintained.

Keep Them Guessing

Children love guessing games. Pique their interest by having them guess the next theme or author you are about to emphasize.

For younger students: The clues must be visual and very obvious. If animal books are the theme of your next study, place stuffed animals or animal pictures around your room.

For older students: Leave clues about the subject or the author around the room. As children find the clues, they may guess the author or the theme. Keep a record of children's responses and give a small reward for a correct guess when the study begins.

Books into Games

Have pupils turn their favorite book into a game. Suppose a group of students want to create a game about Clifford's adventures. Give them index cards and markers. Each draws a picture of a scene from a Clifford book on a card. For each scene they draw, they write a matching sentence or two about it on another index card. To play, all the cards are placed face down on the table. The first player turns over two cards. If he makes a scene and sentence match, he or she keeps those cards and picks two cards again. If the cards don't match, the cards are put back and the next person takes a turn. The winner is the person with the most pairs.

Older children can create a board game. They need to examine a board game they enjoy playing and decide how to adapt it to a book game. They draw the game board on a large piece of poster

...rd liked to run and chase things like the kitten did.

Clifford is my dog. I love give hi...

Clifford was a real hero. He saved the day.

board with "start" and "finish" spots and a segmented road connecting the two. Then children create questions based on one or more books, writing one question on each index card. Borrow a spinner and markers from a commercial game. If a player answers a question correctly, he or she can spin the spinner and move as many places as it says.

Teachers as Book Characters

When introducing a new book or series of books, surprise your students by dressing up as its main character. Wouldn't the children love to see you as Miss Nelson, Amelia Bedelia, or Nate the Great!

Library Buddies

It's great fun to search for good books with a friend. Create pairs of pupils as "library buddies." Encourage them to talk to each other about their reading interests. Ask them to give each other advice about how they choose a book. Then send them to the library to select their books for reading. Change buddies periodically to allow pupils to get different points of view.

Book Bingo

Children enjoy any form of Bingo. This form uses the names of book characters, book titles, authors, and illustrators. Give each pupil a blank card with nine boxes drawn on it and Bingo markers. With the class, generate a list of nine characters, titles, authors, or illustrators on the chalkboard. Then have pupils write them, in any order, on their blank Bingo cards. To play, a caller randomly calls out the names on the list. As a name is called, children put a marker over the box that has that name printed in it. The game continues until someone gets three in a row horizontally, vertically, or diagonally and shouts, "Book Bingo."

Maurice Sendak	Jumanji	Two Bad Ants
Sylvester and the Magic Pebble	Dr. Seuss	Tana Hoban
Millicent Selsam	Hans Christian Anderson	Fish is Fish

READING FOR SPECIAL DAYS AND SEASONS

It's Your Birthday

Make reading a part of pupils' birthdays. Here are some ways.

○ Give each student an inexpensive book for a birthday gift. Of course, it is best if the book is on a topic he or she loves or was written by a favorite author. Write a little inscription in the book. Children will treasure this gift for a lifetime.

○ Have each child write and illustrate a birthday book on his or her birthday. This can include information about the child's life up to the current birthday. Place each completed book in the class library. By the end of the school year, each child's autobiography will be on the shelf. (Children whose birthdays fall over the summer will need to write birthday books at their half birthday or another time.) If you are studying autobiographies, these birthday books make a wonderful starting place.

○ Invite the child who is celebrating a birthday to choose the book that will be read aloud that day. If the child desires, he or she might read the book to the class. Perhaps that child's parent can come to school to read the chosen book to the class.

○ If parents can afford it, encourage them to donate a book to your class library to commemorate their child's birthday. The book can be used, new, or created by the child at home. Create a book plaque to place in each book.

Provide a bibliography to assist parents in their selection. Send home periodically a list of books purchased to avoid duplications.

A special shelf, called the Birthday Book Shelf, can be set aside for these books. The collection will grow as the year progresses. There could also be a special ceremony as the book is placed on the shelf. The birthday child should be given the opportunity to be the first reader of the book that was given.

'Tis the Season To Be Reading . . . Tra La La La La

Any season is *the season* to be reading. Invite pupils to read books that relate to the current season—both fiction and nonfiction. Then plan a seasonal book discussion afternoon when readers bring their book and tell how it relates to the season. If school policy allows, provide treats of the season as discussions take place. In autumn, for instance, cookies shaped as leaves can be given; in winter, cookie snowmen.

Let's Play Ball with Books

Every season has a sport. Connect the sport of the season to books and you have a winning combination. Form class reading teams who compete for the most pages read. Then create a reading progress bulletin board that expresses a sports theme so children can keep track of their reading.

In autumn, football is the game. Determine the length of time for the contest—perhaps the number of weeks between the opening game of the season and the Super Bowl. Each team must "run" 100 yards (or read 1000 pages) to get a touchdown. At the end of the allotted time period, the team with the most touchdowns wins. Each member might receive a book or some other special treat. Don't forget the other teams. They deserve a lesser treat.

In winter, basketball delights its fans. Once again match the length of time to the length of the season. Each team gets *two* points for every basket or, in this case, each book read. Since outside shots gain a player three points in a real basketball game, *three* points can be given for a book with more than 100 pages (or whatever number is appropriate for your group).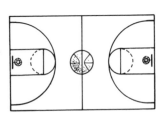

In spring, baseball begins. A base is reached for every book read. Four bases (books) make a run. When the season is over, count up the runs and you'll know the winning team. Prior to the season, decide if very long or mature books could count for two or more bases, perhaps even a home run.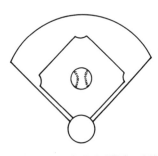

Seasonal Book Awards

Each season has its own special characteristics. Invite children to create Seasonal Book Awards that reflect the spirit of the season. A book whose illustrations depict the fall colors or one whose plot reflects the spirit of Thanksgiving might be a winner. Encourage pupils to be imaginative as they create these awards. Autumn awards could be shaped as leaves. Winter ones could look like snowmen. Spring awards could be flowers or ladybugs. Summer awards could be shaped like a sun. Children should decide the title of the awards. Perhaps one book could win "The Snowy Award" in winter. A spring book could get "The Flower Award." If possible display the books with their awards.

Book Characters at Holiday Time

Who would Ramona send a valentine to on Valentine's Day? What would Mrs. Frisby want for Christmas or Chanukah? What do you think Sarah Noble and her family would have for Thanksgiving dinner?

As each holiday arrives, invite the class to think about the answers to questions like these. Choose a character from a book that you have read as a class. Then pupils can discuss how that character might celebrate the holiday.

SEPTEMBER

Back-to-School with Books

Start the school year off with an enthusiasm for reading. When children arrive, let them discover books in all sorts of places and containers. Perhaps have books hanging from the ceiling, or piled sky high in a reading corner. Why not fill a basket with magazines and a toy sink with books? Give children time to browse through the books. You may wish to read "Clever Book Containers" on page 9 for additional interesting ways to display books.

Opening-Day Book Sharing

Promote reading throughout the year by sharing your love of reading on the very first day of school. Describe your favorite books and ask pupils to tell you about theirs. Encourage them to share what they read during the summer. Was it different from what they read during the school year? Perhaps they read comics or the statistics on the back of baseball cards. Invite children to bring to school and share whatever they enjoyed reading the most.

1st day of school (handwritten annotation)

OCTOBER

Poetry Pause

Try a Poetry Pause on October 15, National Poetry Day. Create a Poetry Pause sign to be held up as an announcement that a poem is about to be read. Then a poem is read aloud. Just as in a Book Break (page 52) everyone stops to listen. You may want to pass out copies of a poem. Children can read along with you or read it at their leisure.

Your class might organize a Schoolwide Poetry Pause. Poetry Pause signs are created for each classroom and one child in each room is chosen to keep it. When Poetry Pause is announced over the public address system, that child holds up the sign and everyone listens as the poem is read.

Physically-Challenged Awareness

National Physically-Challenged Awareness Week is a good time to help pupils develop a sensitivity to the problems handicapped people face. October is a month when children can also develop their awareness of the accomplishments of the handicapped. Expose children to books about those who overcame their handicaps. Such people as Helen Keller, Louis Braille, and Franklin Delano Roosevelt can serve as examples of people who made great accomplishments in their lives. Encourage children to read about these people, using the bibliography on the following page.

Physically-Challenged Awareness Week Bibliography

NONFICTION

Bergman, Thomas, *Finding a Common Language: Children Living with Deafness* (Gareth Stevens Children's Books, 1987)

Bergman, Thomas, *On Our Own Terms: Children Living with Physical Disabilities* (Gareth Stevens Children's Books, 1989)

Rosenberg, Maxine, *My Friend Leslie: The Story of a Handicapped Child* (Lothrop, Lee, & Shepard, 1983)

Sobol, Harriet, *My Brother Steven is Retarded* (Macmillan, 1977)

Wolf, Bernard, *Anna's Silent World* (Lippincott, 1977)

Wolf, Bernard, *Don't Feel Sorry for Paul* (Lippincott, 1974)

FICTION

Younger Readers (K–2)

Cohen, Miriam, *See You Tomorrow, Charles* (Greenwillow, 1983)

Henriod, Lorraine, *Grandma's Wheelchair* (A. Whitman, 1982)

Holcomb, Nan, *A Smile from Andy* (Jason & Nordic, 1989)

Lasker, Joe, *Nick Joins In* (A. Whitman, 1980)

Levi, Dorothy, *A Very Special Friend* (Gallaudet Univ. Press, 1989)

MacLachlan, Patricia, *Through Grandpa's Eyes* (Harper Junior Books, 1980)

Rabe, Bernice, *The Balancing Girl* (Dutton, 1981)

Wannamaker, Bruce, *The Kindness Weapon* (Victor Books, 1984)

Yolen, Jane, *The Seeing Stick* (Harper Junior Books, 1977)

Older Readers (3–6)

Burnett, Frances H., *The Secret Garden* (Penguin, 1987)

Coutant, Helen, *The Gift* (Knopf, 1983)

Garfield, James, *Follow My Leader* (Scholastic, 1987)

Howard, Ellen, *Circle of Giving* (Macmillan, 1984)

Klusmeyer, Joann, *Shelly from Rockytop Farm* (Winston-Derek, 1986)

Madsen, Jane M., *Please Don't Tease Me* (Judson, 1980)

Voigt, Cynthia, *Izzy* (Fawcett, 1987)

Halloween Book Character Creations

It's Halloween and all the goblins are stirring from within their book covers. As Halloween approaches, delight children with stories relating to it. Then let them create a real connection between books and Halloween with this project. Have them create their favorite book characters with a pumpkin, a squash, or Indian corn. Start by asking students to borrow a book from the library depicting the character. Then ask them to think about how they could use a pumpkin, squash, or Indian corn as the base for creating that character. Give each child one of those vegetables plus felt, yarn, fabric scraps, glitter, markers, paint, and so on. Now let the creative process begin.

NOVEMBER

Book Pen Pals

Celebrate National Children's Book Week. Find a class in the same or a different city. As a class write a letter to the children recommending a list of the class's favorite books. Ask that class to respond with a list of its favorite books. Compare the lists. Then have your class try some of the recommended books that were not on your class list.

Feast Your Eyes on Books

In November, many children will have some sort of Thanksgiving celebration. Let them begin by celebrating books. These books can relate to the holiday, or can be about Native North Americans. This is a good time to help pupils enrich their understanding of the role these people played in the life of the early colonists. Children can take these books home to read over the Thanksgiving vacation. Some outstanding titles are listed on the following page.

Native North American and Thanksgiving Bibliography

Aliki, *Corn Is Maize* (Crowell, 1976)

Baker, Betty, *Little Runner of the Longhouse* (Harper Junior Books, 1962)

Baylor, Byrd, *Hawk, I'm Your Brother* (Macmillan, 1976)

Benchley, Nathaniel, *Red Fox and His Canoe* (Harper Junior Books, 1964)

Boegehold, Betty D., *A Horse Called Starfire* (Bantam, 1990)

Celsi, Teresa Noel, *Squanto and the First Thanksgiving* (Raintree, 1989)

Connolly, James, ed., *Why the Possum's Tail Is Bare and Other North American Indian Nature Tales* (Stemmer, House, 1985)

Dalgliesh, Alice, *The Courage of Sarah Noble* (Macmillan, 1987)

Dalgliesh, Alice, *The Thanksgiving Story* (Macmillan, 1985)

dePaola, Tomie, *The Legend of the Indian Paintbrush* (Putnam, 1987)

Farnsworth, Frances Joyce, *Winged Moccasins: The Story of Sacajawea* (Julian Messner, 1954)

Freedman, Paul, *Oh Brother, Oh Friend* (Todd & Honeywell, 1982)

Fritz, Jean, *The Good Giants and The Bad Pukwudgies* (Putnam, 1982)

George, Jean, *The Talking Earth* (Harper Junior Books, 1987)

Goble, Paul, *Buffalo Woman* (Bradbury, 1984)

Goble, Paul, retold by & ill., *Iktomi and the Boulder* (Orchard Books, 1988)

Kessel, Joyce, *Squanto and the First Thanksgiving* (Lerner, 1986)

Kroll, Steven, *Oh, What a Thanksgiving!* (Scholastic, 1988)

Martin, Bill, Jr. & Archambault, John, *Knots on a Counting Rope* (Holt, 1987)

Miller, Montzalee, *My Grandmother's Cookie Jar* (Price Stern Sloan, Inc., 1987)

Parish, Peggy, *Good Hunting Blue Sky* (Harper Junior Books, 1988)

Pomerantz, Charlotte, *Timothy Tall Feather* (Greenwillow, 1986)

Speare, Elizabeth George, *The Sign of the Beaver* (Houghton Mifflin, 1983)

Troughton, Joanna, retold by & ill., *How Rabbit Stole the Fire: A North American Indian Folktale* (Bedrick Blackie, 1986)

Troughton, Joanna, retold by & ill., *Who Will Be the Sun? A North American Indian Folktale* (Bedrick Blackie, 1985)

Ward, Elaine, *The Thanksgiving Feast* (Tabor, 1982)

DECEMBER

Book Greeting Card Gifts

Often adults give books as gifts. We think, "What kind of book would my friend enjoy?" And then we give it. In the same way students can select books as gifts. Ask them to think of a classmate who might enjoy a certain kind of book. Then ask each to make a greeting card that "gives" that book (book suggestion) to the classmate.

Book cards can include:

○ Book name and author
○ A redrawn cover, character, or scene from the book
○ A greeting about the holiday and book, such as "Have Happy Holidays with *Charlotte's Web*."
○ A note with the card about why the child selected the particular book for a classmate. For example, "I know you have a pig collection and thought you'd like reading about Wilbur in this book."
○ The signature of the giving student.

You will want to keep track of who is receiving so that you can "give" book cards to those children who do not seem to be receiving book cards. Or, have the class draw names, so no one is left out.

JANUARY

Caldecott and Newbery Award Month

Celebrate the New Year by reading some of the award-winning books of the previous years. January is the month when the Caldecott and Newbery Medal winners are announced. Use this event to spark interest in these books. To help children understand the significance of these awards, use the activities "Which Books Are Caldecott Medal Winners?" on page 27 and "Read a Newbery Award Winner" on page 30. Attractive posters and pamphlets listing the winners of these medals can be ordered from:

ALA Graphics
American Library Association
50 E. Huron Street
Chicago, IL 60611

Invite a Literacy Volunteer

Invite a literacy volunteer to your classroom on January 8, World Literacy Day. These volunteers can explain the importance of their work as well as describing their job.

FEBRUARY

Reading About Black Heroes

Use the month of January to prepare for Black History Month, which occurs in February. Set aside time to help students increase their understanding of the heritage and cultural contributions of black Americans to our society, though this awareness building should be a natural part of every season and every unit of study. Invite your children to find out more about a black American of their choosing. Here are some people they might want to choose.

Frederick Douglass
Mary McLeod Bethune
Langston Hughes
Kareem Abdul Jabbar
Martin Luther King
Louis Armstrong
Booker T. Washington
George Washington Carver

Scott Joplin
Sojourner Truth
Richard Allen
Harriet Tubman
Phyllis Wheatley
Duke Ellington
Ella Fitzgerald
Hank Aaron

Nat Turner
Crispus Attucks
Marian Anderson
Jesse Owens
Rosa Parks
Paul Robeson
Debi Thomas
Matthew Henson

After reading about each person, the children could write a one-minute message that tells about that person. These messages can be aired during the month of February over the public address system. In addition, students can set up a display about black Americans in the school library. As each message is given, a book about that person can be added to the library display. If you choose to set up this display, have students include information about the display in their announcement.

There are some suggested books for your students on the next page.

Black History Month Bibliography

NONFICTION

Black Americans of Achievement Series published by Chelsea House
   Publishers:

Richard Allen	*Louis Armstrong*
George Washington Carver	*Frederick Douglass*
Duke Ellington	*Ralph Ellison*
Ella Fitzgerald	*Matthew Henson*
Langston Hughes	*Jesse Owens*
Paul Robeson	*Gordon Parks*

Adler, David, *Martin Luther King, Jr.: Free at Last* (Holiday Publishers, 1986)

Davis, Burke, *Black Heroes of the American Revolution* (Harcourt Brace
   Jovanovich, 1976)

Greenfield, Eloise, *Crowell Biography Series—Paul Robeson* (Crowell, 1975)

Mitchell, Barbara, *A Pocketful of Goobers, A Story about George
   Washington Carver* (Carolrhoda Books, Inc., 1986)

Mitchell, Barbara, *Shoes for Everyone, A Story about Jan Matzeliger*
   (Carolrhoda Books, Inc., 1986)

FICTION

Armstrong, William H., *Sounder* (Harper & Row, 1969)

Armstrong, William H., *Sour Land* (Harper & Row, 1971)

Keats, Ezra Jack, *A Letter to Amy* (Harper Junior Books, 1968)

Keats, Ezra Jack, *Peter's Chair* (Harper Junior Books, 1967)

Mathis, Sharon Bell, *The Hundred Penny Box* (Viking, 1975)

Steptoe, John, *Mufaro's Beautiful Daughters: An African Tale* (Lothrop, Lee
   & Shepard, 1987)

Steptoe, John, *Stevie* (Harper Junior Books, 1969)

Taylor, Mildred D., *Roll of Thunder, Hear My Cry* (Dial Books, 1976)

Taylor, Mildred D., *Song of the Trees* (Dial Books, 1975)

Woodson, Jacqueline, *Last Summer with Maizon* (Doubleday, 1990)

A Valentine's Day Book Box

This Valentine's Day Book Box will add another dimension to your class party.

Prior to the day, put slips of paper with two sets of numbers from 1 to 12 (depending on class size) in a container covered with hearts. Each pupil picks a number and finds his or her partner. The pairs of "valentines" then discuss the type of books they like to read and create a list of books they would each enjoy reading.

Divide the class into two groups. Partners cannot be in the same group. Each group visits the school library with the lists of books and pupils choose a book from the list for their partner. Each makes a card for his or her "valentine." It might say "I picked this book especially for you to read. Have a wonderful Valentine's Day!" The card can be attached to the book in the following way.

The books are placed in a box with a giant heart and a label such as: "I AM A BOOK LOVER—BE MINE" or "BE MY BOOK LOVER" or "BOOKS AND LOVE GO TOGETHER FOREVER!"

At the Valentine's Day party, the children will open their books and celebrate. End the party with everyone settling into reading the wonderful Valentine's Day books.

MARCH

March into Spring

March is Music in Our Schools Month. Begin each school day with a little music. Ask students to bring in their favorite records, tapes, and cassettes. Ask students to share what they know about the composer or kind of music. Read aloud or ask students to read aloud information on the record jacket or cassette wrap. Then play the music. Students may want lyrics to some of the songs. These could be written on the board, read as a class, and used as a guide for singing along.

Remarkable Women March into Your Classroom

March (or anytime) is the time of year to recognize the notable women in history. It is National Women's History Month. Encourage children to read biographies of these women to learn about the significant contributions they have made.

Here is a list of some notable women that might interest your students:

Sally Ride	Shirley Chisholm	Emily Dickinson
Grandma Moses	Jackie Joyner-Kersee	Mary Lou Retton
Eleanor Roosevelt	Grace Hopper	Betsy Ross
Dorothy Hamill	Helen Hayes	Susan B. Anthony
Ella Grasso	Eugenie Clark	Clara Barton
Amelia Earhart	Katharine Hepburn	Nelly Bly
Lucy Taylor Hobbs	Elizabeth Blackwell	Margaret Mead
Maria Tallchief	Mary Pickford	Colleen Dewhurst

In addition, there are some books written about great women on the following page.

APRIL

Mathematical Word Problems = Book Solutions

It's Mathematics Education Month. Have children create mathematical word problems about a book they have enjoyed. The problem can involve the characters, the plot, the setting, or the theme. Each writes his or her name and the problem on a sheet of paper, folds up the paper, and places it in a special box. Have a Mathematical Moment session when everyone chooses a question from the box. In turn each tries to answer the word problem and name the book. The child who wrote the word problem checks the answers and tells a little about the book. Some books lend themselves more easily to writing mathematical word problems. There is a list of suggested titles on page 68.

Women's History Month Bibliography

NONFICTION

Women of Our Time Series, published by Viking Kestrel:

Mary McLeod Bethune	*Grandma Moses*
Betty Friedan	*Eleanor Roosevelt*
Dorothea Lange	*Babe Didrikson Zaharias*

American Women of Achievement Series, published by Chelsea House
  Publishers:

Jane Addams	*Lillian Hellman*
Susan B. Anthony	*Anne Hutchinson*
Elizabeth Blackwell	*Clare Boothe Luce*
Nellie Bly	*Barbara McClintock*
Margaret Bourke-White	*Margaret Mead*
Pearl Buck	*Julia Morgan*
Rachel Carson	*Sandra Day O'Connor*
Agnes de Mille	*Wilma Rudolph*
Isadora Duncan	*Phyllis Wheatley*

A Discovery Book Series published by Garrard Publishing Co.:

Abigail Adams	*Dolley Madison*
Jane Addams	*Maria Mitchell*
Clara Barton	*Lucretia Mott*
Dorothea L. Dix	*Florence Nightingale*
Amelia Earhart	*Annie Oakley*
Helen Keller	*Eleanor Roosevelt*
	Narcissa Whitman

McGovern, Ann, *Shark Lady, True Adventures Of Eugenie Clark* (Four
  Winds Press, 1978)

Quackenbush, Robert, *Clear the Cow Pasture I'm Coming in for a Landing!*
  A Story of Amelia Earhart (Simon & Schuster, 1990)

Stevens, Bryna, *Deborah Sampson Goes to War* (Carolrhoda Books)

FICTION

Little, Jean, *Mama's Gonna Buy You a Mockingbird* (Viking, 1985)

MacLachlan, Patricia, *Sarah, Plain and Tall* (Harper Trophy, 1985)

Voigt, Cynthia, *Dicey's Song* (Macmillan, 1982)

Math-Related Children's Literature Bibliography

Anno, Mitsumasa, *All in a Day* (Putnam, 1990)

Anno, Mitsumasa, *Anno's Counting Book* (Crowell, 1977)

Anno, Mitsumasa, *Anno's Counting House* (Putnam, 1982)

Anno, Mitsumasa, *Anno's Math Games* (Putnam, 1987)

Anno, Mitsumasa, *Anno's Mysterious Multiplying Jar* (Putnam, 1983)

Anno, Mitsumasa, *Anno's Sundial* (Putnam, 1987)

Anno, Mitsumasa, *Upside-Downers* (Putnam, 1988)

Carle, Eric, *The Grouchy Ladybug* (Harper Junior Books, 1977)

Carle, Eric, *Pancakes, Pancakes* (Picture Books Studio, 1990)

Carle, Eric, *The Very Hungry Caterpillar* (Putnam, 1981)

Hoban, Tana, *Circles, Triangles, and Squares* (Macmillan, 1974)

Hoban, Tana, *Count and See* (Macmillan, 1972)

Hoban, Tana, *Dots, Spots, Speckles, and Stripes* (Greenwillow, 1987)

Hoban, Tana, *Is It Larger? Is It Smaller?* (Greenwillow, 1985)

Hoban, Tana, *Look! Look! Look!* (Greenwillow, 1988)

Hoban, Tana, *One, Two, Three* (Greenwillow, 1985)

Hoban, Tana, *Over, Under, and Through and Other Spatial Concepts* (Macmillan 1986)

Hoban, Tana, *Round and Round and Round* (Greenwillow, 1983)

Hoban, Tana, *Shapes, Shapes, Shapes* (Greenwillow, 1986)

Hoban, Tana, *26 Letters and 99 Cents* (Greenwillow, 1987)

Hutchins, Pat, *Changes, Changes* (Macmillan, 1987)

Hutchins, Pat, *The Doorbell Rang* (Greenwillow, 1986)

Hutchins, Pat, *1 Hunter* (Greenwillow, 1982)

Hutchins, Pat, *Rosie's Walk* (Macmillan 1968)

Hutchins, Pat, *Titch!* (Macmillan, 1971)

Schwartz, David, *How Much Is a Million?* (Lothrop, Lee, & Shepard, 1985)

Schwartz, David, *If You Made a Million* (Lothrop, Lee, & Shepard, 1989)

MAY

Exercise Your Mind— Read!

May is a good time to stress exercise and physical fitness. Start each day with ten minutes of calisthenics for your body. Match this with ten minutes of reading for your mind. Don't let the connection between the mind and body stop here. Fill your room with books about the human body. There are many pop-up and beautifully illustrated books about the human body. Here's a wonderful chance to use them. Help your students take special notice of the body as a highly efficient machine! Start a trivia bulletin board on which pupils display interesting facts about the body that they find in their reading. For example, the human heart is a pump connected to 100,000 miles of pipelines (arteries, veins).

Mothers in Books

Help your children surprise their mothers with an invaluable gift this Mother's Day—reading a special book to their mother. (If there are children in your class who have no mothers or are not living with this parent, this activity should be avoided.) Bring to class library books in which mothers play an important role. Distribute the books to your class or have pupils make selections. Set aside time for them to practice their reading by reading aloud to each other. As Mother's Day approaches, students will be ready to present their gift. The following page lists some special books that children might enjoy sharing on this holiday.

Mother's Day Bibliography

Younger Readers (K–2)

Bauer, Caroline Feller, *My Mom Travels A Lot* (Live Oak Media, 1982)

Blaine, Mary, *The Terrible Thing That Happened at Our House* (Scholastic, 1983)

Bunting, Eve, *The Mother's Day Mice* (Clarion, 1986)

DeRegniers, Beatrice S., *Waiting for Mama* (Clarion, 1984)

Hallinan, P. K., *We're Very Good Friends My Mother and I* (Childrens, 1989)

Sawicki, Norma, *Something for Mom* (Lothrop, Lee, & Shepard, 1987)

Scott, Ann, *On Mother's Lap* (McGraw Hill, 1972)

Shannon, George, *The Surprise* (Greenwillow, 1983)

Sharmat, Marjorie Weiman, *Horray for Mother's Day!* (Holiday, 1986)

Waber, Bernard, *Lyle Finds His Mother* (Houghton Mifflin, 1974)

Williams, Vera, *A Chair for My Mother* (Morrow, 1988)

Ziefert, Harriet, *Surprise* (Penguin, 1988)

Zindel, Paul, *I Love My Mother* (Harper Junior Books, 1975)

Zolotow, Charlotte, *One Step, Two . . .* (Lothrop, Lee, & Shepard, 1981)

Older Readers (3–6)

Cleary, Beverly, *Ramona and Her Mother* (Morrow, 1979)

Clymer, Eleanor, *My Mother Is the Smartest Woman in the World* (Macmillan, 1982)

Cole, Babette, *The Trouble with Mom* (Putnam, 1986)

Facklam, Margery, *The Trouble with Mothers* (Clarion, 1989)

Greene, Constance, *Star Shine* (Dell, 1987)

Hopkins, Lee B., *Mama* (Knopf, 1977)

Martin, Ann M., *Kristy and the Mother's Day Surprise* (Scholastic, 1989)

Riskind, Mary, *Follow That Mom* (Houghton Mifflin, 1987)

Saroyan, William, *Mama, I Love You* (Dell, 1988)

JUNE

Books Bring Fathers and Children Together

Bring children and their fathers together to read. Prior to Father's Day, have children send home a note like this.

> I love when you READ to me! ☺
>
> Fathers Day is coming soon. Let's read a book together on this special day! I'll bring the book. What time should we read?
> TIME:_____

Encourage children to choose the time with their dads. Children love setting up this special appointment with their fathers. Help children select a book in which fathers play an important role in the story. There are some suggested titles on page 73.

As with the previous activity, if there are children who do not have fathers or do not live with their fathers, this activity should be amended or avoided.

Jump into Summer Reading

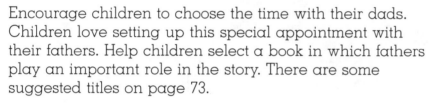

Children love to give suggestions. They feel very important when you ask them to make up summer reading lists for their classmates. Set up cooperative groups for this activity and ask them to focus on books that they feel no one would want to miss. Publish these lists and distribute them just before summer vacation. Children may wish to use one of these catchy titles for their list.

○ Dive into Reading This Summer
○ Sail into Summer with a Book
○ Pack a Book for the Beach
○ Put a Book in Your Picnic Basket

Whatever the title, the results will be the same. Pupils will be thinking about the books they have read and the ones they want to read.

Summer Reading

Here's a very special way to keep children reading all summer. Along with a summer reading list, distribute your school address. As the children complete a book, ask them to write you a letter telling you their reaction to the book. Then write them a little note in response. The idea of communicating with a teacher when there is no school delights children.

Father's Day Bibliography

Younger Readers (K–2)

Caines, Jeannette, *Daddy* (Harper Junior Books, 1977)

Charney, Steve, *Daddy's Whiskers* (Crown, 1989)

Cole, Babette, *The Trouble with Dad* (Putnam, 1986)

Haseley, Dennis, *Kite Flier* (Macmillan, 1986)

Hines, Anna G., *Daddy Makes the Best Spaghetti* (Clarion, 1986)

Horlacher, Bill and Horlacher, Kathy, *I'm Glad I'm Your Dad* (Standard, 1985)

Kroll, Steven, *Happy Father's Day* (Holiday, 1988)

Mayer, Mercer, *Just Me and My Dad* (Western, 1977)

Monjo, F. N., *The One Bad Thing about Father* (Harper Junior Books, 1987)

Ormerod, Jan, *Dad's Back* (Lothrop, Lee, & Shepard, 1985)

Parker, Kristy, *My Dad the Magnificent* (Dutton, 1987)

Steadman, Ralph, *That's My Dad* (Century, Hutchinson, 1987)

Steptoe, John, *Daddy Is a Monster . . . Sometimes* (Harper Junior Books, 1980)

Ziefert, Harriet, *Keeping Daddy Awake on the Way Home from the Beach* (Harper Junior Books, 1986)

Zolotow, Charlotte, *A Father Like That* (Harper Junior Books, 1971)

Older Readers (3–6)

Cleaver, Vera, *Sugar Blue* (Dell, 1986)

Collins, Judith, *Josh's Scary Dad* (Abingdon, 1983)

Dahl, Roald, *Danny: The Champion of the World* (Knopf, 1975)

DeJong, Meindert, *The House of Sixty Fathers* (Harper Junior Books, 1987)

Gifaldi, David, *One Thing for Sure* (Clarion, 1986)

Morris, Judy K., *Crazies and Sam* (Penguin, 1985)

Naylor, Phyllis, *The Keeper* (Macmillan, 1986)

Taylor, Sydney, *A Papa Like Everyone Else* (Dell, 1989)

Thompson, Virginia, *Butch, the Man of the House* (Vantage, 1987)

RESPONDING TO READING

The Performing Book Center

Turn a corner of your classroom into The Performing Book Center where pupils present their reactions to books. These responses are those that an audience would enjoy, for example:

○ reading aloud dialogue from the book
○ presenting a puppet show based on the plot of the book
○ having a debate about the characters
○ dramatizing scenes
○ giving oral editorials
○ expressing opinions and feelings about the book
○ reading aloud a favorite portion of the book
○ presenting original songs or plays created in response to the book

Visual responses to books, like posters, can be used to decorate the center.

Your center should have its own attractive banner that announces its presence. Perhaps a parent would build a small triangular stage an inch or two high that fits neatly into the corner. There should be a special place to display the book related to the performance. A music stand is an ideal device for this. During presentations, classroom chairs can be arranged in front of the center. In some classrooms, children may simply sit on the floor. Once your center is established, make it a permanent part of your room!

Book Banners

Create a "Banner Year" of reading! Banners can be made of muslin, felt, or paper. They can be in any shape or size; they can be elaborate or simple, drawn or collaged. The only must is that the banner relate to a book its creator has read and must contain the title, author, and illustrator

of the book. Attach the banners to dowel sticks or hang them with yarn or ribbon. Decorate your room and nearby halls with these beautiful book banners.

Class Book Flags

Do you have an empty wall in your classroom? Then you have a place for a Class Book Flag. Find a piece of white muslin about three feet by six feet and hang it across your wall at students' eye level. They can write on it and read it during the year. Everyone in the class signs his or her name to the flag, including you. Each time the class or an individual completes a book that is considered worthwhile, the title and author are written on the flag with permanent cloth markers. Add the titles of the adult books you read.

These flags can be hung in a school hall or cafeteria at the end of the school year. After a few years, your school will be filled with Book Flags.

From Book to One-Act Play

Have students transform their favorite fiction book into a one-act play. Here are six steps to guide your students.

1. Choose your favorite part of the plot.
2. List the characters involved.
3. Write the words that the characters would say.
4. Choose classmates to portray each character.
5. Allow time for groups to rehearse.
6. If time permits, create scenery and costumes.

If this project becomes a class activity, it can be presented to other classes, the school, or the community.

Life-Size Book Characters

What could be more fun than creating a three-dimensional life-size model of your class's favorite book character! Develop a frame made from chicken wire and cover with papier-mâché. Whether it be Frances, Ramona, or Mrs. Frisby, the children will love working on their creation. Displaying their sculpture in the front hall of the school will definitely increase the character's popularity and a run on its books. More characters can be added yearly until an "Art Gallery" of book heroes lines your halls.

Simpler life-size book characters can be cut out of large sheets of butcher paper. Children can draw features, glue on features, and mount on a simple wooden frame to make them stand.

A Handful of Clay Book Characters

Clay is a wonderful medium to use for making favorite book characters. The models can fit right into the children's hands. Display clay models of Little Bear, Mousekin, or Charlotte in a showcase with the book. Make other copies of the book available so the "readable moment" isn't lost.

Ready, Set, Cameras, Action

Why not have your own classroom "television station"?

"Welcome to WAVA. Today we will be interviewing the world-famous Winnie the Pooh!"

The interview process allows children to use their higher level thinking skills to create the questions and answers while revealing a deep understanding of the book. It's also a fun-filled interactive method.

For this activity at least two children will have to read the same book. Prior to taping the show, the children plan the interview together. One child is the WAVA interviewer. The other is a character from the book they have read. The questions and their answers must be based on the character's actions, feelings, and thoughts in the book. As they create them, they will develop a greater understanding of the characters in the book. Since this is a television interview, a simple costume for the character and interviewer would make the presentation more realistic. Once the plan is set, allow students time to rehearse the interview before they perform it in front of their class.

If you have the equipment, video-tape the interview and then play it so the class, and the performers, can view it together.

There are many other interviews your students could develop. If children have completed an author study, they can create an interview with that author. One child is the WAVA interviewer, another the author. Once again, interview questions and answers are planned in advance. For an additional twist, have a book character interview the author who created that person or animal. You could even have two characters from the same book interview each other. The possibilities are endless.

Once children become comfortable with the interview process, WAVA will be on the air continually.

Interview question: _____

_____

Possible answers: _____

_____

Interview question: _____

_____

Possible answers: _____

_____

Book Murals, Tapes, Slides, and More

Entertain another class with a unique presentation of a very special book. This experience begins in your classroom as you read aloud a very special book. It could be a picture or storybook or a novel.

Hold discussions about the book throughout the reading. When reading is completed form small groups. Each group chooses a different part of the story to depict in a large mural.

Next ask each group to write a verbal description to accompany its mural. Each group's mural and response can then be put in the correct sequence of the story. You may want to write additional material to connect the scenes. Finally take slide photographs of each mural and tape-record the entire script. Present this talking slide show to another class or give it to the librarian to use with other groups.

Book Character Cards

Some book characters delight the reader. Others inspire them to work harder or achieve more. During the year encourage children to talk about the effect specific book characters have had on them. When a classmate's birthday arrives, ask the others in the class to send cards from the character that is special to the birthday person. They should express the sentiment in the card in the manner that the character would. And of course, have the children share the title and author of the book from which that character comes.

Book Headlines

A newspaper headline says it all. It draws your attention, uses action words, and summarizes what the article is about in a very few words. Bring in and show a few newspaper articles. Cut apart each headline from its

article and display headlines for all to read. Then have each article read aloud. Invite children to identify the headline that belongs with each article. Discuss the elements of the headline as described above. Then students create headlines for the chapter in the book they are currently reading. Or, if you have recently completed reading a class book, invite children to create headlines for different chapters in the book. Read the headlines aloud as everyone tries to guess which chapter it is headlining.

Book Vests

Children love to dress up, especially in things that they have created. Making book vests will delight your class. For this very special project, ask the assistance of parents who enjoy sewing. You will need about one yard of muslin material for each child. Cut out a simple vest from a pattern sized for your students (see page 80). Sew up the side and shoulder seams. Now let the fun begin. When each child reads a book he or she selects a favorite character to draw on the vest. Children draw a brief pencil sketch first, then use fabric crayons or markers for brightly colored results.

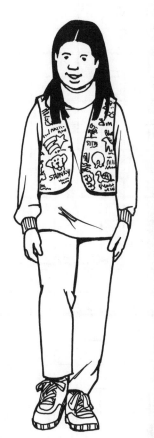

Have a fashion show periodically! As the year progresses, select special days for the students to model their vests for each other and for other classes. As a vest is being modeled the wearer can describe what is on the vest, including the characters and their books. Between fashion shows, vests can be displayed around the classroom.

Photographed Book Talks

Children motivating other children is the result of book talks. Plan special times when pupils present book talks. These talks will enable your students to stand up in front of their peers and discuss a book with confidence. Book talks can take a variety of forms. Here are some popular ways.

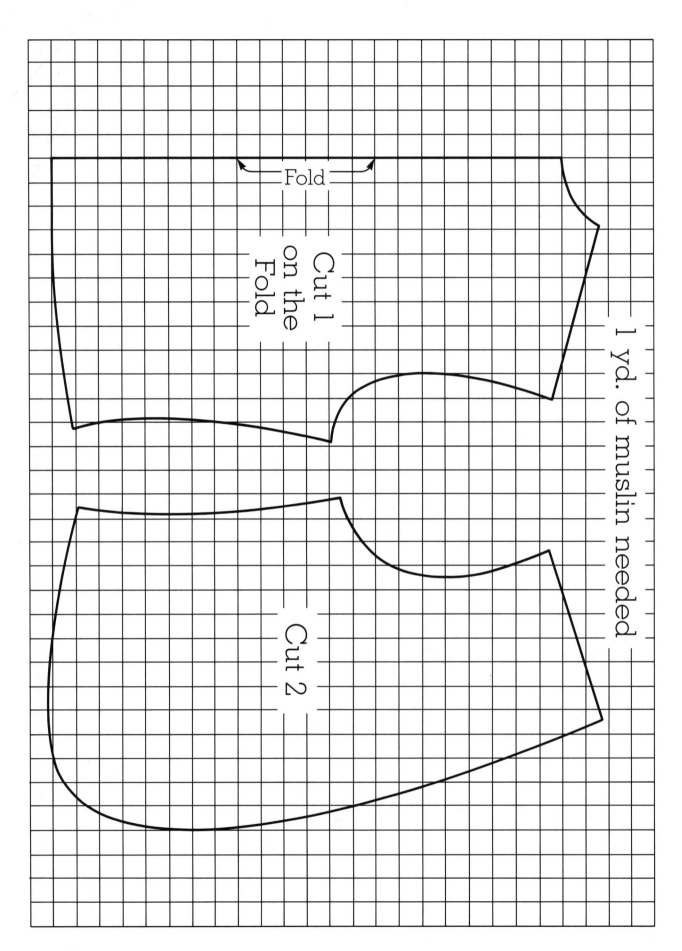

Fold

Cut 1
on the
Fold

Cut 2

1 yd. of muslin needed

○ Dress as a character in the book and tell the things the character did. The costume need not be elaborate.

○ Bring in an artifact and explain its importance to the book. It can be something as simple as a pebble or a necklace.

○ Respond to the book in an artistic manner. Explain your creation.

○ Create simple character puppets and discuss the book with the puppets.

○ Create something that the character in the book made. Explain the creation and how it relates to the book.

After the talk, invite the presenter to answer classmates' questions about the book. As the book talk comes to a close, capture this special moment on film. Then display photographs on a book corner bulletin board.

Book Series Adventure Line

Create an Adventure Line to follow a character through a series of novels. It looks like a time line, but instead of including historical events, it shows the significant events that have occurred in a character's life during the course of a book series.

Ask pupils to create an Adventure Line for their favorite series character. Some of the more popular series are listed on pages 47–48. Have children use long, narrow paper that can be rolled into a scroll. They can cut several sheets of paper into narrow strips and tape them together to form the proper size paper.

Look at this line on page 82 for Laura Ingalls, for example. What exactly did Laura experience as the family moved from the Big Woods to the Prairie? She lived in many places, providing a variety of experiences.

Let children learn to use copyright dates to determine which book in a series came first. Have them create an Adventure Line that shows the time order of experiences. Then have them draw the events or write briefly about the events in the order which they occurred. Include the name of the book in which each experience occurred. Once completed, children can open the scrolls and travel along the Adventure Line.

The Adventures of Laura Ingalls Wilder

Laura was born in Feb. 7, 1867. Laura lived with Ma, Pa, and her sisters Mary and Carrie in a little log house.

THE BIG WOODS

Laura's family traveled to Kansas. Mr. Edwards helped them build the little house. They met friendly Indians. Laura goes to school.

ON THE PRAIRIE

Laura's family moved to Minnesota where they built a new house. Grasshoppers ruin their crop. Laura meets Nellie.

BANKS OF PLUM CREEK

Laura's family moved to the Dakota Territory. Pa went ahead to work in a railroad camp. Grace had been born and Mary was now blind.

SHORES OF SILVERLAKE

Laura's family struggled through a long winter of many blizzards on the prairie. Laura meets Almanzo Wilder.

LONG WINTER

Laura took a job working long hours to pay for Mary to go to college. Laura began studying to be a teacher.

TOWN ON THE PRAIRIE

Laura teaches school. She finds it miserable. Almanzo comes to take her home on weekends.

HAPPY GOLDEN YEARS

Laura marries Almanzo Wilder. Rose is born. Many disasters fill their lives, but they are determined to overcome them.

FIRST FOUR YEARS

Covering the Wall with a Book Scene

The setting of a book creates different images in children's minds. Let their visions appear on the walls of your classroom. Invite children to create their own images of a setting in a book they are reading. Distribute pieces of acetate and washable marker pens to draw with. Project each completed drawing from an overhead projector onto an empty wall or a large screen. While displaying their creations invite the children to describe the scene and where it came from in the book.

A Nonfiction Experience

An interactive bulletin board is an enjoyable way to get children actively involved in reading nonfiction books. Younger children enjoy this project as well.

Have the children write a topic they would like to learn more about on a slip of paper. Then divide the class into small groups based on interest. A trip to the library will allow them to find books on their topic. When reading is done, begin your bulletin board. Help children draw and cut out a large shape that relates to their topic.

Suppose one of your groups has chosen bears as its topic. The cutout would be in the shape of a bear. Draw writing lines across the bear's body and invite pupils to write the facts they have learned about bears. This ongoing experience allows children to write their ideas whenever they are discovered. Display the shapes on the bulletin board and each day spend a few minutes reading the facts from one shape until all have been read.

Create Your Own Bibliography

During the year, children should have read several books that fascinate and/or delight them. Have them create their own bibliographies for these stories. At the end of the year, make a copy of each student's bibliography for the student who will sit in that seat the following year. This will create a special bond between these two students. You may wish to set up a meeting between your new and old students to discuss the books in the bibliography.

Besides sharing a love of books you could use this as an opportunity to teach students to learn correct bibliography form. Use this format to help children understand how to write a bibliography.

Last name of author **comma** First name of author **period** Title **(underlined) period** Place book is published (found on title page) **colon** Publisher (found on title page) **comma** date of publication (found on title page) **period**

Here is the proper bibliographical entry for *Sylvester and the Magic Pebble* by William Steig.

Steig, William. *Sylvester and the Magic Pebble*. New York: Simon and Schuster, Inc., 1969.

Book Quilt

A book quilt makes a beautiful permanent wall hanging in your classroom or a school hall. It brings back fond memories of books that pupils have enjoyed. Follow these steps to create a Book Quilt 48 inches by 72 inches for a class of 24 children. (If your class is larger or smaller, adjust the dimensions accordingly.)

Items you will need to get:

○ three yards of muslin, 45 inches wide
○ one yard of contrasting material, 45 inches wide
○ nine-inch square of heavy cardboard (each child can bring in his or her own)
○ masking tape
○ fabric crayons, permanent markers, or acrylic paint
○ fine-tipped permanent marker

Steps in making:

1. Cut 24 ten-inch squares from the muslin material.
2. Cut 12 two-and-one-half-inch by 45-inch strips from the contrasting material.

3. Tape the muslin to the cardboard with the masking tape. Make sure that the material wraps around the edges and is taped onto the back of the cardboard. This will support the fabric while the child is working on it. It also makes it easy to store the squares until they are done.

4. Each child designs his or her square based on a favorite book. Children can draw directly on the muslin, but it is best if they draw first on a paper the same size. (Children must leave at least one-half inch all around in order to attach the contrasting strips of color described in Step 7.)

5. Pupils use the markers, crayons, or paints to add color to their drawings. Let drawings dry completely.

6. Using a fine-tipped permanent marker, have children write the following on their square:
   ○ name of their favorite book
   ○ their own name
   ○ the date
   ○ perhaps a few relevant notes

7. Sew the strips of contrasting colors between the squares, then sew together to form quilt.

8. Sew more of the contrasting material around the edges as a border.

9. The quilt can be backed with additional muslin if desired.

Your quilt is now ready to be displayed and admired by all. If muslin and sewing are not practical, develop this activity using oak tag and colored poster board—making a paper Book Quilt.

Singing Books

Most children have favorite books and favorite songs. Challenge them to combine the two. Invite children to turn the plot of a book into the lyrics of a song. They can use a tune that is very familiar. Here's the way one child combined the familiar tune of "Three Blind Mice" and the plot of *Caps for Sale* by Esphyr Slobodkina.

"Caps for sale.
Fifty cents each."
He couldn't sell the caps.
He fell asleep.
He woke up and the caps were gone.
The monkeys wore them up in the trees.
"Give me my caps," he screamed and screamed.
"Tsz, Tsz, Tsz."

The peddlar got mad.
He threw his cap down.
He screamed some more.
He looked around.
The monkeys all threw their caps to the ground.
The red and the gray and the blue and the brown.
He put seventeen caps back on his head.
"Caps for Sale."

Books vs. Movies of Books

Some movies have been based on books. For instance, *The Lion, the Witch and the Wardrobe* by C. S. Lewis has been turned into a feature-length animated film. Let children use their higher level thinking skills to compare and contrast the two versions of this novel. To begin, read the book aloud to the class. Discuss the plot, setting, theme, and characters of the book. Then show the film. After the viewing, ask them to analyze the film in the following way.

❍ How are the two versions similar?
❍ How are they different?
❍ Which one did you enjoy more? Why?
❍ Do you think C. S. Lewis would like the film? Why?

Keep Your School Reading

KEEP YOUR SCHOOL READING

Schoolwide Tree of Reading

Get everyone involved in reading. Begin the school year by "planting" a paper tree trunk in the main lobby. This will be the school's Tree of Reading. As children complete a book, they get a leaf to add to the tree. On the leaf they write their name, the title and author of the book they read, and a brief response to the book. When needed, new branches can be added to the tree.

As the seasons change, the tree can change. In autumn, the leaves can be red, brown, yellow, and orange. After covering the tree, they can "fall" to the ground. In winter, the leaves can be replaced by snowflakes filled with book information. In spring, the tree can sprout fresh green leaves. Let the magic of each season bloom on your Tree of Reading.

Audio Cassette Book Readings

With an audio cassette of a book, readers can listen as they follow along in the book. Creating these cassettes is easy to do. All you need is a tape recorder and blank cassettes. Younger pupils can create their own tapes; older ones can make them to share with younger groups. Have pupils choose a book, practice until they can read it expressively, and then tape it.

If older students are taping, they might check with the teacher of a lower grade to see what books would be most popular with that group. The finished tapes can then be presented to the class. "Young" and "old" alike will get great pleasure from the exchange.

A Celebrity-Filled Book Fair

A book fair is an exciting event, but it needs a lot of help from your parent group and much advance planning.

Traditional book fairs display many books that are available for purchase by students and parents for home libraries. If those attending your school would not be in a position to purchase a book, modify the fair to exhibit the library's new books, promote their reading, and perhaps include an appearance from a visiting author or illustrator. Try to arrange it so every child has a chance to see and perhaps speak to this celebrity.

Here are some other activities for your fair:

○ Kick off the fair with a parade of children dressed as book characters.
○ Create class plays, skits, or operettas based on particular books.
○ Decorate the building with murals and other artwork depicting the books by a guest author or illustrator.
○ Display instant photographs of the guest with some of your pupils.

Mini-Book Fairs

Mini-Book Fairs may be more practical for your school. These smaller book fairs celebrate one theme, one or more authors, one grade level. Here are some examples:

○ Celebrate the beginning of each season. All the books displayed or sold are about the season or the holidays that occur during that season.
○ Host a book fair for only one or two grades at a time. All the books at that fair have the appropriate readability.
○ Delight children with a fair dedicated to their favorite authors. *All* the books written by selected authors can be found at this fair.

A Used Book Fair

Calling all unwanted books! Ask pupils to find those books that they haven't read in years, but are still in good condition. Have them bring them to school on a designated day. A committee of adults can screen the books for appropriateness. Then ask for volunteers to help organize the books. Children can decide how to organize the books on display tables—by category, by author, by grade level, or any other reasonable order. Let the children decide how much to charge for each book, and the school Used Book Fair is ready for business. This project will raise money for your school, and at the same time teach children to recycle their used books. This could be done by one or two classes instead of the entire school.

Across the Grades Reading Partners

Reading is an experience that you can share with anyone. Let children experience this firsthand with Across the Grades Reading Partners. A first grader can read to a fifth grader or a fourth grader to a kindergartner. Older children will be wonderfully supportive of younger children who are reading aloud. The younger children are always attentive when that special older child reads to them.

Setting up the program takes planning. Pair up the classes (perhaps a first and a fourth grade), then let the two teachers in each pair create the sets of partners and the places for each set to meet. It would be fun if, on a specific day at a specific time, the entire school could meet with their partners for approximately twenty minutes of reading, but this may not be practical. Probably the two teachers in each pair of classes should set up the times for reading together.

At their meetings, the partners bring their books and decide who will read first. Each should have a chance to read and to talk about the books. The end results are the bonds built between two children and reading.

School Book Store

This is a unique book store. The only way to "buy" something is to read a book(s). Your parent-teacher group might purchase items for the store and keep it maintained.

The criteria for purchases can be decided by teachers, students, or any combination of concerned individuals. Here are some ways to set up a school store.

1. A committee of teachers, librarian, and children can decide which books should be on a recommended list for reading. It can determine how many books must be read before buying something at the store. It may run the store or ask a parent to do so.
2. In each classroom children respond to the books they have read and teachers keep track of the responses.
3. There is a chart that tells how many books must be read in order to purchase each item. Here is a possible chart:

   ○ 1 book = an eraser (the type shaped like an object)
   ○ 2 books = a neon-colored pencil
   ○ 3 books = a yo-yo
   ○ 4 books = a pack of baseball cards
   ○ 5 books = a softcover book

Daily Schoolwide Read-Aloud

Try this unusual idea in your school. Ask your school principal to read for a short period over the public address system. Some principals may feel uncomfortable with the idea at first, but the enthusiasm for reading that it generates will help the project to evolve. As each book is read, it is featured in the school office. In each classroom, there is a poster that lists the books that have been read in this manner. At the end of the year, pupils choose the book they enjoyed the most. That book can be entered into the school Hall of Book Fame. It can proudly be shown in a permanent display case. Each year a copy of the chosen book should be added to the case.

Lunch with the Librarian

What child wouldn't enjoy listening to an award-winning novel? What if it was read by the librarian during lunch? Once you start Lunch with the Librarian, the demand will be endless. Post a sign-up sheet in the cafeteria. Then ask the librarian to choose a group of children from the list to come to the library for a listening lunch once a week. Of course the same group of children eats with the librarian until the book is finished. Then a new group is chosen. If the demand is too great for the librarian to handle alone, organize several small groups and set up a schedule. Each group will be read to by the librarian, a teacher, a parent, or any person interested in the project.

LUNCH AND LISTEN IN THE LIBRARY

Mrs. Ramos invites you to join her on March 8 at 12:00 in the library. Don't forget to bring your lunch. Get ready for an award winning time!

Halloween Book Parade

No more ghosts and witches in your school Halloween parade. This year encourage everyone to come as a favorite book or book character. Among the staff, pick a literature theme. One year it might be fairy tales, the next years folktales, animals, and so on. Teachers should dress up too. Children will be delighted to see their teacher as a favorite book character.

Genre of the Month Club

In this schoolwide activity, children of all grades get together to share their love of reading. Every month a different genre is chosen. Pupils determine which genre they will read by voting. The librarian can help them find books that meet the criteria of the genre and are on their own reading level. The club meets each week to talk about the books and discuss how they demonstrate the qualities of that genre.

Super Storytellers

Invite your students to be traveling storytellers. Children of all ages can retell stories that they have read.

What makes a skilled storyteller? Pose this question. Then tell a story and ask pupils to note the special qualities needed. Here are a few of the needed qualities:

1. Be very familiar with the story.
2. Speak in a voice that can be heard easily.
3. Speak clearly and animatedly.
4. Use different voices for different characters.
5. Make eye contact with the listeners.

Children may want to tell stories individually or in groups. Arrange for storytellers to travel to other classrooms throughout the school to tell their tales.

Books on Wheels

Wouldn't it be fun to share your class's favorite books with other sections of the same grade? Have children collect these books and put them on a mobile cart. Once a week, two or three students wheel the cart to another classroom. While in the room, they promote several of the books by giving mini-book talks, reading a portion of the book aloud, or describing an exciting event.

Children can set up a schedule so they know when it's their turn to wheel the cart. Invite children to decorate the cart with slogans about their books. They might even want to create posters advertising the different selections. Make sure the librarian has copies of the books being promoted so they are available for others to borrow.

Library Sleep-Over

Children like to sleep over at each other's homes. Surprise them by inviting them to a library sleep-over. Let them get out their sleeping bags, collect their favorite books, and bring a flashlight.

You'll need assistance from a group of parents for this exciting event. Children can arrive at the library for a dinner prepared by a group of parents. No more than ten children should attend each book sleep-over. After dinner, let the children share their books around an indoor "campfire," created by crumbling newspapers, putting a few twigs over these papers, then adding crumpled red, orange, and yellow cellophane and a flashlight pointing upwards. Read aloud an appropriate book. The readers can use flashlights to read the books they have brought.

If a sleep-over is not possible, younger chidlren can have a pajama reading party for a part of the evening.

Book Buddies

Book Buddies is an enjoyable way for a pupil to share responses to a book with another child reading the same book. To begin, pair up each child in your class with a child in another class.

Introduce the buddies to one another and let them go to the library to pick out the book they will read. They will need two copies of the same book. Once children have chosen the books, let the reading begin. Set up a schedule so that the buddies can individually read the same book or portion of a book simultaneously.

Book: *Huckleberry Finn* by Mark Twain

Book Buddies	Class	Chapter	Date of Completion
Scott	4-3	1	December 4
Lauren	4-1	1	December 4

After a reading session, each writes or draws a response to the book or book chapter. The responses are placed in envelopes with the buddy's name on it and put in a Book Buddy Mailbox set up in each classroom.

After each reading and responding session, a class Book Buddy Mailperson delivers the envelopes to the other room.

After the Book Buddies have received a few letters from one another, have them get together to discuss and compare their responses to the book.

Periodically assign new buddies and repeat the procedure.

Reading Flavor of the Month

Everyone has a favorite ice cream flavor. Match up an ice cream flavor with a specific genre and you have a delicious book combination. Here are some possible combinations.

Chocolate and Fantasy
Coffee and Poetry
Strawberry and Biography

Vanilla and Tall Tales
Pistachio and Mystery
Peach and Fables

Assign a combination to each month. If during the month, children read the genre of the month, they get a free ice cream in the flavor of the month. Teachers can keep track of the number of children participating in each class. You'll need some help from your parent-teacher group on the last two days of the month.

Prior to the last day, each teacher counts the number of students who participated in the Flavor of the Month and sends the number to the school office where a member of the parent-teacher group gets a total for the school. The correct amount of ice cream can be purchased along with the cones or bowls for it.

On the last day of the month, those children go to the school cafeteria at a specific time of day. There they get their free ice cream and share facts about the books they read. This activity can easily be scaled down to one or two classes.

Hobby Happening

A Hobby Happening gives children a chance to learn more about hobbies and provides them with an opportunity to meet other children who have the same hobby. At the Hobby Happening, each hobby has a table or booth to display materials.

Set up a Hobby Happening for a Friday afternoon. About a month before, invite each child in the school to submit his or her name and hobby. Then organize children into groups based on their hobbies. If possible, have an adult with the same hobby meet with the group. Children can gather reading materials and other things to explain their hobby. For instance, if the hobby is model rocketry, the display might include model rockets, a video tape showing a rocket being ignited and soaring into the air, and an assortment of magazine and newspaper articles, and books about the subject. Some groups might have copies of reading lists about their hobby to hand out. At the Hobby Happening, members of each group take turns manning the table and answering questions about their hobby.

Top Twenty Book Hall of Fame

Here's a project that is best to do in May or June. It provides an opportunity to gather all the students at each grade level together. The ultimate goal is to choose twenty of their favorite books that they read during the school year, for the Top Twenty Book Hall of Fame! To begin, have children work in small groups to generate lists of books. Post the titles for all to see. Discuss all titles submitted by all groups. Next have students create ballots so that everyone in the grade can vote for the top twenty books. Finally the votes can be tabulated for each grade. When the Top Twenty have been chosen, create a large display of these books in a central area. Invite everyone in the school to visit all the displays. Lists can be duplicated and sent home for summer reading. Parents will be interested and appreciative of these student-generated bibliographies.

Hunt and Find

Different books can be found in different rooms of a home. In a kitchen, for instance, one would most likely find cookbooks. But what books would you find in each room of the school? Let pupils brainstorm which books they might find in each room. Here is a sample list that might be generated.

SCHOOLROOM	KINDS OF BOOKS
Art Room	books about artists, how-to-draw books, craft books
Music Room	song books, books on composers
Gymnasium	books about sports, rules of games books
Kitchen	cookbooks
Custodian's Office	books about repairing things
Nurse's Office	books about diseases, books about the human body, first aid books
Main Office	catalogs, address books, phone books
Teacher's Lounge	newspapers, catalogs, magazines, books on teaching ideas

Then take the class on a book hunt through the school and add to the list as the children find new books.

Ask children to look for books in the different rooms of their homes. They might keep a record of the types found in each room. They can bring the lists to school—compare, contrast, and tally them.

Book Surveys

Everyone has a favorite book. How many other people have the same favorite book? Take a survey and you'll find the answer. Let children begin in the classroom, by learning everyone's favorite book. Each writes the title of his or her favorite book. Then count the votes. Keep a tally on a posted chart. List each book and put a check each time the title is read an additional time. After you have surveyed the class, continue on to the grade, the school, or even the school district. Keep the chart visible. Encourage your students to choose a title from the list when they are searching for a new book.

Another year try this survey with favorite authors, illustrators, or even characters. This project creates an ongoing awareness of books.

Rainbow Search

Red, yellow, orange, blue, green, indigo, and violet. Have a schoolwide rainbow book search. Display a large rainbow in the main hallway, titled "Books Color Our World." Ask pupils to search for fiction books that have one of those colors as the primary color of the book jacket. Then decorate your rainbow by hanging student-created book jackets of these books on the appropriate color.

Famous Animals Hall of Fame

Children love to read stories about animals. Create a Famous Animals Hall of Fame. Set up a schoolwide (gradewide, or simply class) committee to meet on a regular basis to create this Hall of Fame. To begin, it establishes criteria for nominating candidates. Here are some character traits that children may wish to consider: courage, generosity, kindness, strength, and intelligence. The committee then posts the criteria and invites everyone in the school to nominate animal characters from books. The committee creates the ballots, passes them out to each class, and tabulates

the results. The winners are announced over the public address system. Finally the committee creates a bulletin board display of the winning animals in the main hallway of the school. Don't be surprised to see such characters as Arthur, Clifford, Lyle the Crocodile, Charlotte, Wilbur, Sounder, Tuck, and the Velveteen Rabbit appear in your Hall of Fame.

Principals Participate

The principal is a special person in your school building. Perhaps he or she has a special hobby that would interest students. Can she perform magic tricks? Perhaps she is a dancer or a singer. What would pupils have to do to get him or her to perform? Perhaps read a certain number of books in a certain period of time. Approach your principal. If he or she says "Yes" then spread the word. Pupils will be motivated to read the required number of books to see their principal perform. Teachers keep track of the number of books read in their classrooms. When the school reaches the required amount, the performance begins. Children will be delighted to see their principal in this new light.

A Book Count

How many books do you think there are in the school library? Let children estimate. Record their estimates. Next divide the class into groups. You may want to have fiction, nonfiction, biography, easy reader, and other groups for counting. Have them start counting the number of books in the library, keeping a tally of the count. At the end of the search, add up everyone's amounts. The children can compare their totals with the original estimates. They can also compare the number of fiction versus nonfiction books.

The Scavenger Hunt

Children like to hunt for things. Why not connect a hunt to a book? Set up a scavenger hunt for one or more classes. Let them search for items related to a book. Weather permitting, use the school playground. If this is not possible, hide the items in two or three rooms, or throughout the school. Set up teams. Then give each a list of items to be found and a time limit. Within the given amount of time, the children must search for the items on their list. The team that brings back the most items wins the scavenger hunt. After the hunt, display all the items. Then gather everyone around you while you read the book. As an item is mentioned in the book, find it on the display and show it.

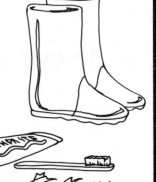

My Father's Dragon by Ruth Stiles Gannett is a wonderful book to use for a scavenger hunt. In this story, Elmer gets a variety of objects from a wise cat that allow him to rescue the baby dragon from the wild animals of the island. Here are some items pupils could hunt for:

- ○ chewing gum
- ○ a compass
- ○ a toothbrush and a tube of toothpaste
- ○ a package of rubber bands
- ○ a comb and hairbrush
- ○ a pair of black rubber boots
- ○ six magnifying glasses
- ○ seven hair ribbons of different colors
- ○ two dozen pink lollipops

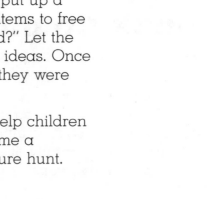

Once pupils have found all of Elmer's things, put up a sign that says, "Guess how Elmer uses these items to free the baby dragon from the beast of Wild Island?" Let the children work with a partner to come up with ideas. Once you read them the book, they will discover if they were correct.

NOTE: You may choose to make up clues to help children locate the objects. Then this activity will become a combination of a scavenger hunt and a treasure hunt.

The "All Eyes on Reading" Newsletter

How exciting it would be to publish a schoolwide newsletter devoted entirely to books. To do this, you will need an intergrade committee that is commited to this project and an interested supervising adult. Your school librarian would be a perfect candidate for this supervisory position if he or she has the time. Each grade could

contribute articles about favorite books, book characters, authors, and illustrators. Some children could become "famous" book critics. Here are some features you may wish to have in the newspaper:

○ A column devoted to an update on the most popular books in each class.
○ Feature articles on classroom activities based on books, written by the children.
○ News reports detailing the adventures of famous characters.
○ Headlines announcing the arrival of new books to the school.
○ Reports on sports heroes in books pupil writers have read.
○ Jokes, riddles, and puzzles about famous books.
○ A page highlighting reviews of movies made from books
○ Letters to the editor, written by "book characters."
○ A "Food for Thought" page of recipes from particular books.
○ Student-written "ads," advertising favorite books with illustrations included.

Give your newsletter a catchy name like "All Eyes on Reading." Publish and circulate the newsletter every other month. Watch how excited the school becomes on the day it is distributed.

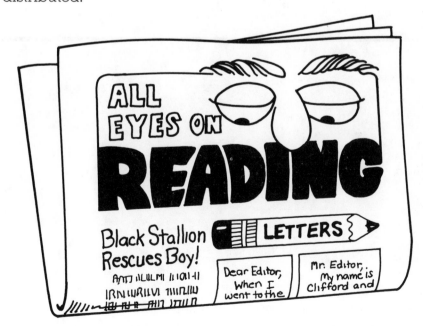

Keep Your Community Reading

KEEP YOUR COMMUNITY READING

Bring a love of reading to your community. This chapter presents specific activities to promote sharing, learning, and understanding that reading is a part of everyone's life. Encourage adults to demonstrate that reading is part of their lives. Let children know that the world outside of school is filled with reading material.

Family Read-Aloud

What better way to encourage reading, than to read as a family? The school can assist this by periodically sending home short book lists on specific topics—the seasons, current topics in the news, sports, classics, such adult books as *Blue Highways* by William Least Heat Moon, and so on. The family can take turns reading aloud. A love of reading can be established during this kind of sharing activity.

Spread the Joy of Reading

Help children realize that it is a gift to be able to read by taking them to a local center for the blind or to a nursing home that has blind residents. Have them read aloud to these people. Either prior to or during the trip, show pupils books written in Braille or in large type print. If such a trip is impossible, let the children experience the Braille and large print books by bringing copies into the classroom. Help children conclude that one reason the Braille system and large print books exist is because of people's desire to read.

Extended Family Reading in School

What a nice experience to share a book with a favorite grandparent, uncle, or aunt! Plan a special time when pupils can invite a member of their extended family to the classroom for a special family reading. You might want to send out invitations.

> Please join us for a day of family reading fun.
> Would you bring a book to read from?
>
> Date: _____
>
> Place: _____
>
> Time: _____

When the adults arrive, the children greet them, and each pupil and relative pair finds a special spot to read together. Plan to have other people around to read with those pupils who do not have a relative present. After everyone has shared the personal books, call everyone together as you read excerpts from one of these books about special relationships between children and their families. (See the Grandparents Bibliography on page 105.)

A welcoming banner and refreshments would make the event even more spectacular.

NOTE: If your school is in an area where reading could take place outdoors, then you might want to plan this day for the warmer weather.

Adult Sections in the Library

Reading is a form of pleasure for many adults. Help pupils begin to learn about the world of books for adults by showing them that world. Take a class trip to your local library. Ask the librarian to give your group a tour of the different areas of the library that adults use. Then divide the class into groups. Each group has a hands-on experience browsing through one section to see the different types of reading material there.

Survey: Parents and Childhood Books

Ask pupils to talk to their parents about their childhoods. Suggest they take notes about parents' early reading experiences. Did someone often read to them? Did they

Grandparents Bibliography

Younger Readers (K–2)

Adler, David, *A Little at a Time* (Random, 1976)

Aliki, *The Two of Them* (Greenwillow, 1979)

Berger, Barbara, *Grandfather Twilight* (Putnam, 1988)

Brandenberg, Franz, *A Secret for Grandmother's Birthday* (Greenwillow, 1985)

Bunting, Eve, *The Wednesday Surprise* (Clarion, 1989)

Carlstorm, Nancy, *Grandpappy* (Little, Brown, & Co., 1990)

Caseley, Judith, *Apple Pie and Onions* (Greenwillow, 1987)

Caseley, Judith, *When Grandpa Came to Stay* (Greenwillow, 1986)

dePaola, Tomie, *Nana Upstairs and Nana Downstairs* (Putnam, 1973)

dePaola, Tomie, *Now One Foot, Now the Other* (Putnam, 1981)

Flournoy, Valerie, *The Patchwork Quilt* (Dial, 1985)

Fox, Mem, *Shoes from Grandpa* (Orchard Books, 1989)

Gelfand, Marilyn, *My Great Grandpa* (Macmillan, 1986)

Greenfield, Eloise, *Grandpa's Face* (Putnam, 1988)

Hedderwick, Mairi, *Katie Morag and the Two Grandmothers* (Little, Brown, & Co., 1986)

Hickman, Martha, *When James Allen Whitaker's Grandfather Came to Stay* (Abingdon, 1985)

Hines, Anna, *Grandma Gets Grumpy* (Clarion, 1988)

Hooker, Ruth, *At Grandma and Grandpa's House* (Whitman, 1986)

Keller, Holly, *The Best Present* (Greenwillow, 1989)

Knox-Wagner, Elaine, *My Grandpa Retired Today* (Whitman, 1982)

Kroll, Steven, *Annie's Four Grannies* (Holiday, 1986)

Kroll, Steven, *If I Could Be My Grandmother* (Pantheon, 1977)

Levison, Riki, *Watch the Stars Come Out* (Dutton, 1985)

McCully, Emily, *The Grandma Mix-Up* (Harper Junior Books, 1988)

MacLachlan, Patricia, *Through Grandpa's Eyes* (Harper Junior Books, 1983)

Martin, Bill, Jr. and Archambault, John, *Knots on a Counting Rope* (Holt, 1987)

Nelson, Vaunda, *Always Grandma* (Putnam, 1988)

Root, Phyllis and Marron, Carol, *Gretchen's Grandma* (Raintree, 1983)

Williams, Barbara, *Kevin's Grandma* (Dutton, 1975)

Yolen, Jane, *No Bath Tonight* (Harper Junior Books, 1978)

Older Readers (3–6)

Carlson, Natalie, *A Grandmother for the Orphelines* (Harper Junior Books, 1980)

Gaedert, LouAnn, *A Summer Like Turnips* (Holt, 1989)

Greenfield, Eloise, *Grandmama's Joy* (Putnam, 1980)

Griffith, Helen, *Grandaddy's Place* (Greenwillow, 1987)

Hicks, Clifford, *Pop and Peter Potts* (Holt, 1984)

Holl, Kristi, *Just Like a Real Family* (Macmillan, 1983)

Nixon, Joan, *The Gift* (Macmillan, 1983)

Patterson, Nancy, *The Christmas Cup* (Watts, 1989)

Smith, Robert, *The War with Grandpa* (Delacorte, 1984)

Streich, Corrine, ed., *Grandparents' Houses: Poems about Grandparents* (Greenwillow, 1984)

read to themselves? What kinds of books did they like to read—sports, nonfiction, fiction, science fiction, and so on? Can they remember titles they especially enjoyed? Were any of them books that are still being read today? Do they have any of these books? Perhaps pupils can bring one or more of these books to class. (Some may be in another language.) Remind students that these books are someone else's treasures and should be treated accordingly.

From pupils' notes, compile a class list of book topics or titles that were most popular with parents. Are they the same interests of pupils today? Children may be surprised to learn how close are their interests and those of their parents.

Read to Your Parent Tonight

Once a week have "Read to Your Parent Tonight" night. During the school day, each child chooses a book or book chapter to read to his or her parent that night. After reading, suggest pupil and parent talk about favorite parts, least favorite parts, most exciting incident, and so on. Children might find out if their parent would like them to bring home another book by the same author. Children will truly enjoy leading this discussion with their parents at home.

Older students will most likely choose to share chapters of books. They might read one chapter each evening, followed by a chapter by chapter discussion, culminating in a discussion evaluating their feelings about the entire book.

Bridge the Generations with Books

Books can bring the generations together. Match up your students with senior citizens in the community. You may contact seniors at a local retirement home or local community senior programs. Invite them to come to your classroom to share books with your students.

Students create invitations for the senior citizens that include the date, time, and place. It might suggest that they bring a book that they enjoyed when they were little, or one they think pupils would like. You might also send along a grade level list of books that can be found at the local library.

Plan the time the seniors are in the classroom so all guests have a chance to tell why they think the books they brought would appeal to your group. Experiencing a book through the mind of a senior citizen will be a memorable experience for pupils.

Older students will enjoy this different way of bringing the generations together. Choose one book for the seniors and your students to read. It should be a book that has stood the test of time, like *Peter Pan, Alice in Wonderland, The Red Badge of Courage, Black Beauty.* Or, it could be a current popular novel. Prior to the meeting the seniors and the students read the book. On the meeting day, they can share their views and discuss their reactions to the book.

A Reading Tour of Town

Reading is part of our everyday lives. Help children note this by taking them on a field trip to a shopping area. As children walk down the street or through a mall, encourage them to read every printed word they see. Children will delight one another by the continuous reading of words. "Strawberries on Sale," "Going Out of Business Sale," "One Way," "Bob's Book Store" are some of the words you'll hear.

On the return trip home, discuss with children the problems that someone who can not read might encounter.

Help for Adults Who Are Learning English

Does your community have people for whom English is not their first language? Contact a group that helps the adults learn English and ask how your children might help. Here are some projects that you might undertake:

○ Have the children make simple books to teach English. These books can be one word with a picture drawn under it.

○ Explain to students that many of these adults have children they would like to read to. Have the children visit the library. Encourage them to choose books that people who can barely read English might be able to read to their children. Compile a list of these books and send them to the agency.

○ Arrange with the agency for older students to read to a person just learning English. The reading visits could take place at the school or at the agency.

Pack-a-Book

This activity brings a new excitement to reading at home. Prepare a backpack filled with a special book, plus drawing paper, markers, crayons, scissors, glue, lunch-size paper bags for puppets, scraps of cloths, and any other art material useful for a simple art project about the book. Include a set of directions for the project plus a letter to parents inviting them to participate as listeners of the reading. Child and parent read the book, complete the project, and return the backpack in the allotted time. Of course the longer the book, the longer the time given, but do not include a book that will take more than three evenings to read and respond to. Otherwise the enthusiasm in the classroom is lost. Send the backpack home with a different child each night by picking a name from a hat. As soon as everyone has had a turn, change the book and activity to keep children interested.

The children will clamor to get their turn to take home the backpack! Keeping everything secretive until the last person has taken the pack home makes it even more enticing.

Read-a-Thon

Plan a Read-a-Thon to raise money for your school library. Here is how to set it up. Give each child a Read-a-Thon sponsor sheet (page 111). He or she determines the minimum number of pages to read during that month

and writes that number on the sheet. In this way the sponsor will know the minimum amount of money they will be pledging.

Then children take the Read-a-Thon sponsor sheet home and ask adults to sponsor their reading during the given month. Once they return the sheets to school, the reading begins!

During the month, the children read, then complete the Read-a-Thon Recommendation Sheet (page 112). You may need to reproduce several of these for each student. They enter the title, author, number of pages, and recommendation for each book they read. The recommendation should be brief but must include information that reflects that they actually read the book. Teachers or parents should periodically check to make sure that the recommendations do this. Children should also understand that these recommendations will be used to choose new books that will be bought for the library. After the month of reading is complete, the children take their pledge sheet back to the sponsors to collect the money.

The Read-a-Thon Recommendation Sheets are handed to a committee of students, parents, and teachers. This committee then reads the recommendations. The books most heavily recommended and with the best reviews will be put on a possible purchase list. The amount of money raised will determine how many of these books might be purchased.

Book Theme Carnival

What better way to promote books than to have a school carnival based on books? Each class or grade sets up a game or food booth that has a book theme. Getting parents involved is a must. If you have class mothers or fathers they can be responsible for the booth for each class or grade. Involve the children in creating the booths. The booths can be as complex as setting up a race track for radio control cars or as simple as tossing a ball through an opening. Or students might opt to sell food at their booth. Here are some carnival booths that have worked well:

Race a car around the land of *Jumanji.*
Toss the ball through *A Wrinkle in Time.*
Throw the water balloon at *Miss Nelson.*
Go fishing with *Kermit, the Hermit Crab.*
Eat pasta with *Strega Nona.*

Booths can be set up in the school gym or outside if the weather is good. Excitement will fill the school on carnival day! Parents and children can take turns manning the booths. Game tickets, for perhaps $.25 each, can be sold as people enter the school. People use a ticket to play a game or eat at a carnival booth. In addition, you can sell copies of the book being highlighted at each booth. The money raised can be used to buy more books for the school library.

Places To Relax and Read at Home

Reading in a cozy place adds something special to the experience. To encourage children to read at home, ask them to survey their homes for the places in which they like to read. Here are some of the places that they may discover: under the bed covers, on a window seat, in a comfortable chair, under a tree, in a clubhouse, in a tree house, on a blanket, in the back of the family car. Have them share their ideas with their classmates. Encourage children to try different places during the coming weeks. Then invite them to share their reactions. Watch your room fill with discussions about the best cozy places to read.

Read-a-Thon
Sponsor Sheet

Name _____

Class _____

School _____

Minimum number of pages to read _____

Sponsor	Address	Amount pledged $__ × number of pages	Number of pages read
_____	_____	_____	_____
_____	_____	_____	_____
_____	_____	_____	_____
_____	_____	_____	_____
_____	_____	_____	_____
_____	_____	_____	_____
_____	_____	_____	_____
_____	_____	_____	_____
_____	_____	_____	_____
_____	_____	_____	_____
_____	_____	_____	_____
_____	_____	_____	_____
_____	_____	_____	_____
_____	_____	_____	_____
_____	_____	_____	_____
_____	_____	_____	_____

Read-a-Thon
Recommendation Sheet

Name _____

Class _____

School _____

Title of Book _____

Author _____ # of pages _____

This book is rated: ☐ Not to be missed!   ☐ Entertaining

☐ Enjoyable   ☐ O.K.   ☐ Boring

Recommendation: Should this book be bought for the school library? Why or why not? _____

_____

_____

_____

Title of Book _____

Author _____ # of pages _____

This book is rated: ☐ Not to be missed!   ☐ Entertaining

☐ Enjoyable   ☐ O.K.   ☐ Boring

Recommendation: Should this book be bought for the school library? Why or why not? _____

_____

_____

_____